# Mastering
# Spanish Irregular Verbs

# Mastering
# Spanish Irregular Verbs

### A Simplified Approach and Visual Guide to Achieving Spanish Verb Fluency

**For Intermediate and
Advanced Students**

by

**Juan M. González, Ph.D.
Dan Bishop, Ph.D.**

iUniverse, Inc.
New York   Bloomington

**Mastering Spanish Irregular Verbs**
**A Simplified Approach and Visual Guide for Spanish Verb Fluency**

*iUniverse books may be ordered through booksellers or by contacting:*

*iUniverse*
*1663 Liberty Drive*
*Bloomington, IN 47403*
*www.iuniverse.com*
*1-800-Authors (1-800-288-4677)*

*ISBN: 978-1-4401-1536-3 (pbk)*
*ISBN: 978-1-4401-1776-3 (cloth)*
*ISBN: 978-1-4401-1777-0 (ebk)*

*Library of Congress Control Number: 2009922689*

*Printed in the United States of America*

*iUniverse rev. date: 02/ 6/2009*

To our wives, whose patience, support and gracious understanding helped make this book possible.

# Contents

# Preface

While studying Spanish and teaching this wonderful language to English–speaking students, one major hurdle to overcome is the difficulty associated with learning Spanish verbs. Conjugating verbs in six persons and fourteen tenses is a completely novel experience for English speakers. Add to that the frustration in dealing with the seemingly endless jungle of irregular Spanish verbs. Some verbs have oddities in the present tense, others in the preterit. Some verbs that contain the letter "o" change this vowel to "ue" in some tenses, while others do not. The list seems endless.

This problem is compounded by the simple fact that mastering a language is often a fragmented process taking place over a lengthy period of time. The instructor may cover the present tense in September and not introduce the preterit until November, while putting off the conditional tense till spring semester or later and postponing the subjunctive tenses until the second year of study. Thus it becomes difficult for the student to see the forest for the trees.

To address these issues, we first set out to devise an organizational scheme that would simplify the morass of verb irregularities by creating categories to which verbs that display similar characteristics could be assigned. In doing so, we were able to generalize verb irregularities into three main groupings: irregularities due to iron-clad spelling rules, irregularities caused by vowel changes within the verb itself, and a small group of renegade verbs that we have labeled Truly Irregular Verbs. We have thus reduced the mountain of irregularities to three easily managed mole hills consisting of ten spelling rules, ten variations in vowel structure, and nineteen Truly Irregular Verbs.

In order to present these patterns most effectively, we make each irregularity itself, rather than the verb tense, the starting point, and we demonstrate how that irregularity affects the six forms in each of the seven simple tenses and the two participles. In addition, we include comprehensive verb lists for each category of irregularity in both chapters 3 and 4 to help identify exactly which verbs exhibit a particular irregular conjugation pattern.

With this approach, we believe that students of Spanish will become comfortable dealing with verb irregularities much earlier in their studies. This in turn will lead to achieving a higher degree of fluency more quickly than is possible using traditional methods.

# Introduction

Irregular verb conjugations are often the biggest hurdle that foreign language students must face. It seems as if half of the verbs have some form of irregularity waiting to trip up the student. Yet a mastery of irregular verbs is necessary to achieve any respectable degree of fluency.

Nearly a third of all Spanish verbs have some variation in one or more of their tense conjugations. It comes as no surprise that beginning and intermediate students often feel frustrated when dealing with Spanish verbs. Yet the task of gaining control over Spanish irregular verbs is far easier than it looks. The majority of so-called irregularities can be categorized into a small number of easily managed groups, leaving a mere nineteen verb families that are the real renegades: the Truly Irregular Verbs. This book will simplify your study of Spanish verbs and greatly enhance your ability to recognize and deal with irregularites as they arise in your readings and conversation.

Chapter 1 outlines our general approach to verb conjugation while providing a quick review of the seven simple tenses. This chapter provides an important frame of reference for the material in the following chapters, so **it is critical that you review Chapter 1 before proceeding**, regardless of your current skill level.

Chapters 2 through 4 tackle verb irregularities in a unique format using conjugation charts alongside examples, adding a visual element to the learning process. We believe this makes the task of mastering irregular Spanish verbs much more manageable. We introduce ten iron–clad spelling rules that apply without exception to all verbs (and all other parts of speech as well). We then present ten variations in vowel structure, some more common than others, which affect many Spanish verb conjugations.

Only nineteen verbs (and their families) remain to be characterized after the spelling rule and vowel variation categories have been applied. (A verb family is a group of verbs that share the same verb root. For example, **contener, sustener, detener** all belong to the **tener** family and are all conjugated identically.) These are labeled the Truly Irregular Verbs, and a complete chapter has been assigned to deal with these nineteen verbs individually, highlighting similarities in their conjugations to simplify their mastery.

We have adopted the following conventions and abbreviations: 1S, 2S, and 3S followed by a verb tense refer to the first, second and third person singular forms for the specified tense. Similarly 1P, 2P, and 3P refer to the first, second and third person plural forms. Tense abbreviations are as follows:

| Pr |
|----|
| **1S** |
| |
| |
| **Im** |
| |
| |
| **Pret** |
| |
| |
| **F / C** |
| |
| |
| **P S** |
| 1S 1P |
| 2S 2P |
| 3S 3P |
| **I S** |
| |
| |

| | | |
|-----|-----|-----|
| Pr | ⇨ | Present Tense |
| Im | ⇨ | Imperfect Tense |
| Pret | ⇨ | Preterit Tense |
| F | ⇨ | Future Tense |
| C | ⇨ | Conditional Tense |
| PS | ⇨ | Present Subjunctive Tense |
| IS | ⇨ | Imperfect Subjunctive Tense |

Where we wish to emphize particular forms of a verb that are affected by a spelling rule or variation in form, we present a conjugation diagram such as that shown at the left. This diagram consists of two columns of blocks: the column on the left for singular forms and the column on the right for plural forms. We have combined the future and conditional tenses, since they share the same base and whatever affects one affects the other.

Those forms that are affected by the change under discussion are darkened. The example shown indicates that the 1S-present and all six of the present subjunctive forms are affected by the rule under discussion.

The following table format represents the conjugation construction of a verb in its seven simple tenses. For tenses that follow regular conjugation, we present only the 1S form for that tense and the box for that tense is shaded. For tenses having irregular conjugations, we show all six forms of the verb for the irregular tense and the box for that tense remains white. Any feature that requires special identification is also highlighted in white. The examples below illustrate this convention for **hablar**, *to speak*, a perfectly regular Spanish verb, and for **nacer**, *to be born*, which has spelling irregularities in its present and present subjunctive tenses.

**hablar,** *to speak*

Pres.Part: **hablando**          Past Part: **hablado**

| Pres: | Pret: | Fut: |
|-------|-------|------|
| hablo | hablé | hablaré |
| Imp: | | Cond: |
| hablaba | | hablaría |
| Pres.Sub: | | Imp.Sub: |
| hable | | hablara (hablase) |

**nacer,** *to be born*

Pres.Part: **naciendo**          Past Part: **nacido**

| Pres: | | Pret: | Fut: |
|---|---|---|---|
| nazco | nacemos | nací | naceré |
| naces | nacéis | | |
| nace | nacen | | |
| Imp: | | | Cond: |
| nacía | | | nacería |
| Pres.Sub: | | Imp.Sub: | |
| nazca | nazcamos | naciera | |
| nazcas | nazcáis | (naciese) | |
| nazca | nazcan | | |

Note that since the imperfect subjunctive tense in Spanish has two alternative constructions, we show the 1S form for both alternatives, with the less common form in parentheses.

# Chapter 1

## Regular Verb Conjugation I:
## The Seven Simple Tenses

This chapter demonstrates our approach to constructing verb forms in the various conjugations while providing a quick summary and review of the conjugation patterns for Spanish verbs. Even if you feel comfortable with verb conjugation, you must spend a few moments studying the material in this chapter, as it will provide the foundation you will need for the material that follows. This method is simpler than others that you may have previously encountered. Also, by reviewing all tenses at once in a single short chapter, you will see relationships between the different constructions that you might not have noticed before, allowing you to create some mnemonic devices of your own that will help you in your everyday use of the Spanish language.

## Two Verb Types

The infinitive form for all Spanish verbs ends in –**ar**, –**er**, or –**ir**, making verbs easy to recognize. For example:

| | |
|---|---|
| **hablar** | *to speak* |
| **comer** | *to eat* |
| **abrir** | *to open* |

Few words other than verbs have these endings.

Most Spanish language courses teach that there are three types of Spanish verbs, based on the infinitive endings. However, the –*er* and the –*ir* verb types have identical conjugation patterns throughout all fourteen tenses with only three exceptions.

We can simplify the learning of Spanish verb conjugations by combining the –*er* and –*ir* verb types into a single type, the –*er/–ir* verbs, and memorizing the three exceptions to their otherwise identical conjugation patterns.

# Spanish Verb Construction

The Spanish language has fourteen common verb tenses: seven simple single–word constructions and seven compound tenses made by using a form of the verb **haber**, *to have,* along with the past participle of the desired verb.

Each tense has six separate verb forms, based on the verb's subject. That is, six different verb forms are used depending on whether the subject is I, he/she/it/you (sing.), we, they/you (pl.), you (familiar, sing.), or you (familiar, pl.). The term "conjugation" refers to the listing of the six verb forms associated with a given tense for a particular verb. For example, the conjugation of **hablar**, *to speak*, in the present tense is:

| | | | |
|---|---|---|---|
| **hablo** | *I speak* | **hablamos** | *we speak* |
| **hablas** | *you speak* | **habláis** | *you speak* |
| | *(familiar, sing.)* | | *(familiar, pl.)* |
| **habla** | *he/she/it speaks* | **hablan** | *they speak* |
| | *you (sing.) speak* | | *you (pl.) speak* |

For all regular verbs, each specific verb form is constructed by adding an appropriate ending to a base, or root, that is closely related to that verb's infinitive. For example:

| Infinitive | ⇨ | Base | + | Ending | = | Desired Verb |
|---|---|---|---|---|---|---|
| **hablar** | ⇨ | **habl–** | + | **–amos** | = | **hablamos** |
| (to speak) | | | | | | (we speak) |

For the imperfect and conditional tenses, an additional linking unit is inserted between the appropriate base and the ending. There are only two links used in Spanish conjugations: **–ab–** and an accented **–í–**. For example:

| Infinitive | ⇨ | Base | + | Link | + Ending | = | Desired Verb |
|---|---|---|---|---|---|---|---|
| **hablar** | ⇨ | **habl–** | + | **–ab–** | + **–amos** | = | **hablábamos** |
| (to speak) | | | | | | | (we spoke) |

Thus:

Imperfect Tense

| | | |
|---|---|---|
| **hablábamos** | ⇨ | *we spoke* |
| **comíamos** | ⇨ | *we ate* |

Conditional Tense

| | | |
|---|---|---|
| **hablaríamos** | ⇨ | *we would speak* |
| **comeríamos** | ⇨ | *we would eat* |

Except for the small group of Truly Irregular Verbs we shall deal with later, you will encounter only four bases throughout all Spanish verb conjugations, to which are assigned the letters B1, B2, B3, and B4.

Finally, there are only four ending groups to learn, which are designated as the A–endings, E–endings, pA–endings, and pI–endings.

We'll begin by reviewing the four bases that form the foundation for all Spanish verb forms.

## Four Bases

**Base B1** is formed by dropping the –**ar**, –**er**, or –**ir** ending from the infinitive. This base is used for the present, imperfect and preterit tenses. Thus:

| Infinitive | | | Base B1 |
|---|---|---|---|
| **hablar** | *to speak* | ⇨ | **habl–** |
| **comer** | *to eat* | ⇨ | **com–** |
| **abrir** | *to open* | ⇨ | **abr–** |

**Base B2** is the unchanged infinitive. In essence, to use the B2 base, the appropriate ending is simply added to the infinitive. The future and conditional tenses use the B2 base.

| Infinitive | | | Base B2 |
|---|---|---|---|
| **hablar** | *to speak* | ⇨ | **hablar–** |
| **comer** | *to eat* | ⇨ | **comer–** |
| **abrir** | *to open* | ⇨ | **abrir–** |

**Base B3** is used only by the present subjunctive tense. It is formed by dropping the –**o** or –**oy** ending from the 1S–present form of the verb. If the verb is regular, the B3 ending is identical to the B1 ending.

| Infinitive | | | 1S-Present | | Base B3 |
|---|---|---|---|---|---|
| **hablar** | *to speak* | ⇨ | **hablo** | ⇨ | **habl–** |
| **comer** | *to eat* | ⇨ | **como** | ⇨ | **com–** |
| **abrir** | *to open* | ⇨ | **abro** | ⇨ | **abr–** |

However, if there are any spelling changes or vowel variations in the 1S–present, those changes appear in the B3 base and affect some or all of the present subjunctive forms for that verb. The examples below illustrate this situation.

| Infinitive | | 1S-Present | | Base B3 |
|---|---|---|---|---|
| contar | *to count* | ⇨ cuento | ⇨ | cuent– |
| caer | *to fall* | ⇨ caigo | ⇨ | caig– |
| freir | *to fry* | ⇨ frío | ⇨ | fri– |

**Base B4** is used only by the imperfect subjunctive tense. It is constructed from the 3P–preterit form of the verb and is formed by dropping the **–on** from the 3P–preterit ending. For regular *–ar* verbs, this results in a base that looks the same as the B2 base (that is, the infinitive itself). For example:

| Infinitive | | 3P-Preterit | | Base B4 |
|---|---|---|---|---|
| hablar | *to speak* | ⇨ hablaron | ⇨ | hablar– |
| comer | *to eat* | ⇨ comieron | ⇨ | comier– |
| abrir | *to open* | ⇨ abrieron | ⇨ | abrier– |

However, if the verb exhibits a spelling change or variation in the 3P–preterit form, that change or variation also appears throughout the imperfect subjunctive via the B4 base. The examples below illustrate this situation.

| Infinitive | | 3P-Preterit | | Base B4 |
|---|---|---|---|---|
| andar | *to walk* | ⇨ anduvieron | ⇨ | anduvier– |
| caer | *to fall* | ⇨ cayeron | ⇨ | cayer– |
| dormir | *to sleep* | ⇨ durmieron | ⇨ | durmier– |

There is an alternative form of the imperfect subjunctive in which the B4 base is formed by dropping the **–on** from the 3P–preterit form and replacing the final **–r–** with an **–s–**. Both alternatives are commonly encountered in literature and in certain regions of the Spanish speaking world, so it is well to become familiar with both. For example, using the six verbs shown above, we have:

| Infinitive | | 3P-Preterit | | Alt. Base B4 |
|---|---|---|---|---|
| hablar | *to speak* | ⇨ hablaron | ⇨ | hablas– |
| comer | *to eat* | ⇨ comieron | ⇨ | comies– |
| abrir | *to open* | ⇨ abrieron | ⇨ | abries– |

and

| | | | | | |
|---|---|---|---|---|---|
| **andar** | *to walk* | ⇨ | **anduvieron** | ⇨ | **anduvies–** |
| **caer** | *to fall* | ⇨ | **cayeron** | ⇨ | **cayes–** |
| **dormir** | *to sleep* | ⇨ | **durmieron** | ⇨ | **durmies–** |

## Four Ending Groups

Spanish verb conjugations have four different ending groups which we are designating as A–endings, E–endings, pA–endings, and pI–endings. Do not confuse A–endings and E–endings with the *–ar* and *–er/–ir* verb types. As you will see shortly, both verb types utilize both of these ending groups for the various tenses. The table below shows the A–endings and the E–endings.

| **A–endings** | | | **E–endings** | |
|---|---|---|---|---|
| 1S: –a | 1P: –amos | | 1S: –e | 1P: –emos |
| 2S: –as | 2P: –ais | | 2S: –es | 2P: –eis |
| 3S: –a | 3P: –an | | 3S: –e | 3P: –en |

As you can see, the two groups match each other in all six forms, differing only in the first letter of each ending. Also note that the 1S and 3S forms are the same in each of the two groups.

The preterit tense has its own two ending groups, the pA–endings and the pI–endings (the preceding "p" standing for preterit). In this case, the pA–endings are used only in the preterit conjugation of the *–ar* verb type, and the pI–endings are used only in the preterit conjugation of the *–er/–ir* verb types.

The following table shows the pA–endings and the pI–endings that are used only with the preterit tense.

| **pA–endings** | | | **pI–endings** | |
|---|---|---|---|---|
| 1S: –é | 1P: –amos | | 1S: –í | 1P: –imos |
| 2S: –aste | 2P: –asteis | | 2S: –iste | 2P: –isteis |
| 3S: –ó | 3P: –aron | | 3S: –ió | 3P: –ieron |

Note that the 1S–preterit and 3S–preterit for both ending groups are accented on the final vowel. For *–ar* verbs, this accent on the final –ó is often the only distinction between 3S–preterit and 1S–present since both tenses use the B1 base. One of the distinguishing characteristics of the Truly Irregular Verbs is the complete absence of accents in all of the preterit forms.

Also note that for *–ar* verbs both the pA–ending group and the A–ending group have the same 1P ending, **–amos**, so for most *–ar* verbs the 1P–present and 1P–preterit are identical. Distinguishing between them in actual practice relies entirely on the context in which the verb is used.

Another useful observation is that all of the pI–endings begin with the letter **–i–**.

## Two Linking Units

As mentioned earlier, only two tenses require a linking unit between the base and the ending. These are the imperfect and the conditional tenses.

The imperfect tense uses an **–ab–** link for the *–ar* verbs and an accented **–í–**link for the *–er/–ir* verbs.
Thus you have:

**Ella hablaba rápidamente.**
*She spoke rapidly.*
**El perro comía siempre por la tarde.**
*The dog always ate in the afternoon.*

The conditional tense uses the accented **–í–** link for all verbs regardless of type. For example:

**Le ayudaría si ella me pidiera.**
*I would help her if she asked.*
**Me gustaría hablar contigo**.
*I would like to speak with you.*
**Huiría antes que me pudieran encontrar.**
*I would flee before they could find me.*

With these building blocks in hand, the four bases, four ending groups, and two linking units, we are now ready to tackle the construction of Spanish verbs in all seven of their regular simple tenses.

# The Present Tense

---

**B1 base + A–endings (–*ar* verbs) or**
**E–endings (–*er*/–*ir* verbs)**
**with 3 notable exceptions**

---

The present tense is formed by adding the A–endings to the B1 base for the
–*ar* verbs and the E–endings to the B1 base for the –*er*/–*ir* verbs, with the
following three important exceptions.

**THREE EXCEPTIONS to the A–ending and E–ending
conjugation patterns for the present tense:**

1. For ALL but four Truly Irregular Verbs (**ser**, **estar**, **dar**, and
   **ir**) the 1S–present form ends in –**o** rather than –**a** or –**e**.

2. The 1P–present for ALL –*ir* verbs has –**imos** as the ending
   rather than –**emos**.

3. The 2P–present for ALL –*ir* verbs has –**ís** (accented) as the
   ending rather than –**éis**.

These three exceptions are highlighted in white in the example tables
below.

**hablar** *to speak*

| 1S | hablo | 1P | hablamos |
|----|-------|----|----------|
| 2S | hablas | 2P | habláis |
| 3S | habla | 3P | hablan |

**comer** *to eat*

| 1S | como | 1P | comemos |
|----|------|----|---------|
| 2S | comes | 2P | coméis |
| 3S | come | 3P | comen |

**abrir** *to open*

| 1S | abro | 1P | abrimos |
|----|------|----|---------|
| 2S | abres | 2P | abrís |
| 3S | abre | 3P | abren |

Exceptions 2 and 3 (and a seldom used form covered in the section on command forms) are the ONLY places where the forms for *–er* verbs and *–ir* verbs differ throughout their entire conjugations in all tenses.

Note that for almost all verbs, the 2P form has an accent over the first vowel in the ending for the present tense. Knowing the accent marks is an important part of learning verb conjugations in Spanish. Not only do they help in pronouncing the word correctly, but in many cases the accent mark is the only element that differentiates a verb form in one tense from its form in another. For example:

**Hablo**. *I am speaking. (present tense)*
**Habló**. *She spoke. (preterit tense)*

# The Imperfect Tense

---

**B1 base** + **–ab–** link (*–ar* verbs) + **A–endings** or
**–í–** link (*–er/–ir* verbs) + **A–endings**

---

The imperfect tense, like the present tense, uses the B1 base. All verbs use the A–endings in the imperfect tense, regardless of type. The *–ar* verbs require the **–ab–** link between the B1 base and A–ending, while the *–er/–ir* verbs require the accented **–í–** link between the B1 base and the A–ending.

Also note that for the *–ar* verbs in the 1P–imperfect, the vowel in the **–ab–** link is accented.

| **hablar** *to speak* | | | |
|------|-----------|----|------------|
| 1S | hablaba | 1P | hablábamos |
| 2S | hablabas | 2P | hablabais |
| 3S | hablaba | 3P | hablaban |

| **comer** *to eat* | | | |
|------|---------|----|-----------|
| 1S | comía | 1P | comíamos |
| 2S | comías | 2P | comíais |
| 3S | comía | 3P | comían |

| **abrir** *to open* | | | |
|------|---------|----|-----------|
| 1S | abría | 1P | abríamos |
| 2S | abrías | 2P | abríais |
| 3S | abría | 3P | abrían |

# The Future Tense

---

## B2 base + mix of E–endings and A–endings

E–endings

| | |
|---|---|
| **1S** | **1P** |
| **2S** | **2P** |
| **3S** | **3P** |

A–endings

All verbs are conjugated similarly in the future tense. The future tense endings draw from a mixture of the E–endings and the A–endings. The diagram to the left and the charts below illustrate how this mixing works. The 1S, 1P, and 2P forms all use E–endings (black cells), while the 2S, 3S, and 3P forms use A–endings (white cells).

The ending is attached directly to the B2 base, which is the unchanged infinitive form of the verb. All of the endings *except* 1P are accented, just the opposite of the imperfect tense.

| **hablar** *to speak* | | | |
|---|---|---|---|
| 1S | hablaré | 1P | hablaremos |
| 2S | hablarás | 2P | hablaréis |
| 3S | hablará | 3P | hablarán |

| **comer** *to eat* | | | |
|---|---|---|---|
| 1S | comeré | 1P | comeremos |
| 2S | comerás | 2P | comeréis |
| 3S | comerá | 3P | comerán |

| **abrir** *to open* | | | |
|---|---|---|---|
| 1S | abriré | 1P | abriremos |
| 2S | abrirás | 2P | abriréis |
| 3S | abrirá | 3P | abrirán |

# The Conditional Tense

---

**B2 base  +   –í– link   +   A–endings**

---

All verbs are conjugated similarly in the conditional tense. Like the future tense, the conditional tense uses the B2 (infinitive) base, and, like the imperfect tense, ALL verbs use the A–endings. ALL verbs require the use of the accented –í– as a link between the B2 base and the A–ending. Thus all verb types are treated alike in the conditional tense.

| **hablar** *to speak* | | | |
|------|------------|-----|---------------|
| 1S | hablaría | 1P | hablaríamos |
| 2S | hablarías | 2P | hablaríais |
| 3S | hablaría | 3P | hablarían |

| **comer** *to eat* | | | |
|------|------------|-----|---------------|
| 1S | comería | 1P | comeríamos |
| 2S | comerías | 2P | comeríais |
| 3S | comería | 3P | comerían |

| **abrir** *to open* | | | |
|------|------------|-----|---------------|
| 1S | abriría | 1P | abriríamos |
| 2S | abrirías | 2P | abriríais |
| 3S | abriría | 3P | abrirían |

Note that for the 2S, 3S, and 3P forms, the accented –í– link in the conditional and the accented ending in the future are the only differences between the conditional and future forms of the verb. For example:

> **hablará**    *she will speak*
> **hablaría**   *she would speak*

Be careful not to confuse the imperfect and the conditional tense forms for –er/–ir verbs. The same link is used and the 2S, 3S, and 3P endings are the same. However, the imperfect tense uses the B1 base (with the ending dropped from the infinitive), while the conditional uses the B2 base (the infinitive), so the forms never match. For example:

> **comían**    *they ate*
> **comerían**  *they would eat*

# The Preterit Tense

---

**B1 base** + **pA–endings** (*–ar* **verbs) or**
**pI–endings** (*–er/–ir* **verbs)**

---

The preterit tense has its own set of endings for each of the two verb types: the pA–endings and the pI–endings. The preterit uses the B1 base, to which the pA–endings are attached for the *–ar* verbs and the pI–endings are attached for the *–er/–ir* verbs.

| **hablar** *to speak* | | | |
|------|-----------|-----|-------------|
| 1S | hablé | 1P | hablamos |
| 2S | hablaste | 2P | hablasteis |
| 3S | habló | 3P | hablaron |

| **comer** *to eat* | | | |
|------|-----------|-----|-------------|
| 1S | comí | 1P | comimos |
| 2S | comiste | 2P | comisteis |
| 3S | comió | 3P | comieron |

| **abrir** *to open* | | | |
|------|-----------|-----|-------------|
| 1S | abrí | 1P | abrimos |
| 2S | abriste | 2P | abristeis |
| 3S | abrió | 3P | abrieron |

Pay special attention to the 3P forms (shaded in the tables above). This form provides the root for the B4 base (by dropping the **–on** ending), which is used by the imperfect subjunctive tense.

| 3P–preterit | B4 Base | Alt. B4 Base |
|-------------|---------|--------------|
| **abrieron** *they opened* ⇨ | **abrier–** | **abries–** |

# The Present Subjunctive Tense

---

**B3 base  +  E–endings (*–ar* verbs) or**
**A–endings (*–er/–ir* verbs)**

---

The present subjunctive tense uses the B3 base (formed from the 1S–present by dropping the –**o** ending). Any irregularities in the 1S–present are carried over into the B3 base. For example:

| Infinitive | | 1S-present | | B3 Base |
|---|---|---|---|---|
| **hablar** | *to speak* | ⇨ **hablo** | ⇨ | **habl–** |
| **caer** | *to fall* | ⇨ **caigo** | ⇨ | **caig–** |

For this tense, the *–ar* verbs use the E–endings and the *–er/–ir* verbs use the A–endings. This is just the reverse of the present tense endings. As in the present tense, the 2P forms are accented.

It should be noted that even though a verb may have an irregular 1S–present form that then affects the present subjunctive through the B3 base, in most cases the present subjunctive is still conjugated following the rules stated here. In that sense, the present subjunctive itself is not irregular.

| **hablar** *to speak* | | | |
|---|---|---|---|
| 1S | hable | 1P | hablemos |
| 2S | hables | 2P | habléis |
| 3S | hable | 3P | hablen |

| **comer** *to eat* | | | |
|---|---|---|---|
| 1S | coma | 1P | comamos |
| 2S | comas | 2P | comáis |
| 3S | coma | 3P | coman |

| **abrir** *to open* | | | |
|---|---|---|---|
| 1S | abra | 1P | abramos |
| 2S | abras | 2P | abráis |
| 3S | abra | 3P | abran |

# The Imperfect Subjunctive Tense

---

**B4 base + A–endings**
 **or alternatively**
**B4 base with –s– replacing the final –r– + E–endings**

---

There are two different ways to form the imperfect subjunctive. Both use the 3P–preterit to form the B4 base by dropping the –**on** ending from that form. Any irregularities in the 3P–preterit are carried over into the B4 base. For example:

| Infinitive | | | 3P-preterit | | B4 Base |
|---|---|---|---|---|---|
| **hablar** | *to speak* | ⇨ | **hablaron** | ⇨ | **hablar–** |
| **caer** | *to fall* | ⇨ | **cayeron** | ⇨ | **cayer–** |

  The more common construction takes the B4 base and adds the A–endings to it, resulting in the following examples:

| **hablar** *to speak* | | | |
|---|---|---|---|
| 1S | hablara | 1P | habláramos |
| 2S | hablaras | 2P | hablarais |
| 3S | hablara | 3P | hablaran |

| **comer** *to eat* | | | |
|---|---|---|---|
| 1S | comiera | 1P | comiéramos |
| 2S | comieras | 2P | comierais |
| 3S | comiera | 3P | comieran |

| **abrir** *to open* | | | |
|---|---|---|---|
| 1S | abriera | 1P | abriéramos |
| 2S | abrieras | 2P | abrierais |
| 3S | abriera | 3P | abrieran |

The alternative method for constructing the imperfect subjunctive modifies the B4 base by replacing the final –r– with an –s–, and then attaches the E–endings to the resulting altered base. This results in the following examples:

| Infinitive | | 3P-preterit | | Alt. B4 Base |
|---|---|---|---|---|
| hablar | *I speak* ⇨ | hablaron | ⇨ | hablas– |
| caer | *I fall* ⇨ | cayeron | ⇨ | cayes– |

Alternate Form:

| **hablar** *to speak* | | | |
|---|---|---|---|
| 1S | hablase | 1P | hablásemos |
| 2S | hablases | 2P | hablaseis |
| 3S | hablase | 3P | hablasen |

Alternate Form:

| **comer** *to eat* | | | |
|---|---|---|---|
| 1S | comiese | 1P | comiésemos |
| 2S | comieses | 2P | comieseis |
| 3S | comiese | 3P | comiesen |

Alternate Form:

| **abrir** *to open* | | | |
|---|---|---|---|
| 1S | abriese | 1P | abriésemos |
| 2S | abrieses | 2P | abrieseis |
| 3S | abriese | 3P | abriesen |

All imperfect subjunctive conjugations have an accent in the 1P form located on the syllable *before* the –**amos** or –**emos** ending.

Any irregularity that shows up in the 3P–preterit of a verb is carried over into the imperfect subjunctive conjugations through the B4 base. In most cases the imperfect subjunctive is conjugated regularly using the rules outlined in this section, in spite of having the irregular base. Thus learning the irregularity in the 3P–preterit for such verbs will give you all you need to know to conjugate the imperfect subjunctive properly.

---

**By recognizing that a tense may be conjugated in a completely regular fashion in spite of its irregular base, you will have simplified your study of Spanish irregular verbs considerably.**

---

# The Imperative (Command) Forms

The imperative forms in Spanish use the present subjunctive tense, with two notable exceptions. For the 2S and 2P forms (the familiar "you" forms) Spanish distinguishes between negative commands (Don't move!) and affirmative, or positive, commands (Sit!). The 2S and 2P *negative* commands use the corresponding present subjunctive forms. However, the 2S and 2P affirmative commands follow different rules (see below).

Furthermore, the 1S command form is never used. Presumably, if you were to talk to yourself and give yourself a command, you would use either the **tú** or the **usted** command form as though the command were coming to you from a different person.

The 1P–command form (**nosotros**) uses the 1P–present subjunctive in both affirmative and negative connotations. However, since we don't "command" ourselves (we always command others), this form has a different interpretation, as illustrated in these examples:

**Quedemos como amigos.** *Let's remain friends.*
**No vayamos.** *Let's not go.*
**¡Comamos!** *Let's eat.*

The 3S–command form (**usted**) uses the 3S–present subjunctive for both positive and negative commands.

**Abra la ventana por favor.** *Please open the window.*
**No abra la caja hoy.** *Don't open the box today.*

The 3P–command form (**ustedes**) uses the 3P–present subjunctive for both positive and negative commands.

**Siéntense por favor.** *Please take your seats.*
**No se levanten por favor.** *Please don't get up.*

This leaves the 2S and 2P command forms, which have two different endings, depending on whether the command is negative or affirmative.

The 2S–command form (**tú**) uses the 2S–present subjunctive form *for negative commands only.*

**No abras la caja hoy.** *Don't open the box today.*

The 2P–command form (**vosotros**) uses the 2P–present subjunctive form *for negative commands only.*

    **¡No tiréis la arena!.**    *Don't throw sand!*

For the 2S–command form (**tú**) for affirmative commands, use the 3S–present form of the verb. Thus:

    **¡Habla!**    *Speak!*
    **¡Come!**    *Eat!*
    **¡Toma tu leche!**    *Drink your milk!*

For the 2P–command form (**vosotros**) for affirmative commands, use the B1 base and add either **–ad**, **–ed**, or **–id**, depending on whether the verb is an *–ar*, *–er*, or *–ir* verb.

This is the only verb form that ends in a **–d**. Note also that this form is the third exception to the rule that *–er* and *–ir* verbs share identical conjugations.

    **¡Salid de vuestro trabajo!**    *Leave your work!*
    **Niños, estudiad con mucha diligencia**
        *Children, study with great diligence.*

The following tables will help you remember which forms to use. The only forms that do not use the present subjunctive tense, the 2S and 2P affirmative commands, are shaded.

### *–ar* **Verbs**

| Affirmative Commands | | | |
|------|------|------|------|
| 1S | not used | 1P | 1P–present subj.<br>**¡hablemos!** |
| 2S | 3S–present<br>**¡habla!** | 2P | B1 base + **–ad**<br>**¡Hablad!** |
| 3S | 3S–present subj.<br>**¡hable!** | 3P | 3P–present subj.<br>**¡hablen!** |

| Negative Commands | | | |
|------|------|------|------|
| 1S | not used | 1P | 1P–present subj.<br>**¡No hablemos!** |
| 2S | 2S–present subj.<br>**¡No hables!** | 2P | 2P–present subj.<br>**¡No habléis!** |
| 3S | 3S–present subj.<br>**¡No hable!** | 3P | 3P–present subj.<br>**¡No hablen!** |

### *–er* **Verbs**

| Affirmative Commands | | | |
|------|------|------|------|
| 1S | not used | 1P | 1P–present subj.<br>**¡Comamos!** |
| 2S | 3S–present<br>**¡Come!** | 2P | B1 base + **–ed**<br>**¡Comed!** |
| 3S | 3S–present subj.<br>**¡Coma!** | 3P | 3P–present subj.<br>**¡Coman!** |

| Negative Commands | | | |
|------|------|------|------|
| 1S | not used | 1P | 1P–present subj.<br>**¡No comamos!** |
| 2S | 2S–present subj.<br>**¡No comas!** | 2P | 2P–present subj.<br>**¡No comáis!** |
| 3S | 3S–present subj.<br>**¡No coma!** | 3P | 3P–present subj.<br>**¡No coman!** |

## –*ir* Verbs

| Affirmative Commands | | | |
|------|------|------|------|
| 1S | not used | 1P | 1P–present subj. **¡Inscribamos!** |
| 2S | 3S–present **¡Inscribe!** | 2P | B1 base + –**id** **¡Inscribid!** |
| 3S | 3S–present subj. **¡Inscriba!** | 3P | 3P–present subj. **¡Inscriban!** |

| Negative Commands | | | |
|------|------|------|------|
| 1S | not used | 1P | 1P–present subj. **¡No inscribamos!** |
| 2S | 2S–present subj. **¡No inscribas!** | 2P | 2P–present subj. **¡No inscribáis!** |
| 3S | 3S–present subj. **¡No inscriba!** | 3P | 3P–present subj. **¡No inscriban!** |

# The Present and Past Participles

The present and past participles are used extensively in Spanish, so it is important to recognize them and to construct them properly. You will frequently find the present participle combined with an auxiliary verb to express progressive or continuing action. The past participle is used with the auxiliary verb **haber,** *to have,* to form all seven of the compound tenses.

---

Present Participle:
**B1 base** + –ando   (*–ar* **verbs**) or
         –iendo   (*–er/–ir* **verbs**)

---

| | | |
|---|---|---|
| hablar | *to speak* ⇨ | **hablando** |

**Estaremos hablando mañana.**
> *We are going to speak tomorrow.*

| | | |
|---|---|---|
| comer | *to eat* ⇨ | **comiendo** |

**Él estaba comiendo la manzana**
> *He was eating the apple.*

| | | |
|---|---|---|
| asir | *to sieze* ⇨ | **asiendo** |

**Ellos estaban asiendo la bandera.**
> *They were siezing the flag.*

---

Past Participle:
**B1 base** + –ado   (*–ar* **verbs**) or
         –ido   (*–er/–ir* **verbs**)

---

| | | |
|---|---|---|
| hablar | *to speak* ⇨ | **hablado** |

**Ella ha hablado a los niños.**
> *She has spoken to the children.*

| | | |
|---|---|---|
| comer | *to eat* ⇨ | **comido** |

**Nosotros ya habíamos comido.**
> *We had already eaten.*

| | | |
|---|---|---|
| asir | *to grasp* ⇨ | **asido** |

**¿Han asido la soga aún?**
> *Have you grasped the rope yet?*

# Regular Verb Conjugation I: Summary

Four bases are used to form the seven simple tenses:

**Base B1**: Drop infinitive's –**ar**/–**er**/–**ir** ending.

**Base B2**: Use the unchanged infinitive.

**Base B3**: Drop the –**o** or –**oy** from the 1S–present form.

**Base B4**: Drop the –**on** from the 3P–preterit form or,
alternatively, drop the –**on** from the 3P–preterit
and replace the final –**r**– with an –**s**–.

Four ending groups are added to the base (or base + link) to create the final verb form. Two of these, the pA– and pI–endings, are used only for the preterit tense.

| A–endings | | E–endings | |
|---|---|---|---|
| 1S: –a | 1P: –amos | 1S: –e | 1P: –emos |
| 2S: –as | 2P: –ais | 2S: –es | 2P: –eis |
| 3S: –a | 3P: –an | 3S: –e | 3P: –en |

| pA–endings (for preterit) | | pI–endings (for preterit) | |
|---|---|---|---|
| 1S: –é | 1P: –amos | 1S: –í | 1P: –imos |
| 2S: –aste | 2P: –asteis | 2S: –iste | 2P: –isteis |
| 3S: –ó | 3P: –aron | 3S: –ió | 3P: –ieron |

Two tenses require a linking unit between the base and the ending.

Imperfect Tense: Linking unit for –*ar* verbs:  –**ab**–
Linking unit for –*er*/–*ir*  verbs:  accented –**i**–

Conditional Tense: Linking unit for ALL verbs:  accented –**i**–

| Tense | Verb Type | Base & Link | Ending : Examples |
|---|---|---|---|
| Pres. | –*ar* | B1 | A–endings except for –**o** in 1S:<br>**hablo, hablas**... |
| | –*er*/–*ir* | B1 | E–endings except for –**o** in 1S:<br>**como, comes**...<br>and, for –*ir* verbs:<br>1P : –**imos**: **asimos**<br>2P: –**ís**: **asís** |
| Imp. | –*ar* | B1+ –**ab**– | A–endings: **hablaba**... |
| | –*er*/–*ir* | B1+ –**í**– | A–endings: **comía**...<br>**asía**... |
| Pret. | –*ar* | B1 | pA–endings: **hablé, hablaste**... |
| | –*er*/–*ir* | B1 | pI–endings: **comí, comiste**...<br>**así, asiste**... |
| Fut. | ALL | B2 | E & A mix endings: **hablaré**...<br>**comeré**...<br>**asiré**... |
| Cond. | ALL | B2+ –**í**– | A–endings: **hablaría**...<br>**comería**...<br>**asiría**... |
| PrSub. | –*ar* | B3 | E–endings: **hable, hables**... |
| | –*er*/–*ir* | B3 | A–endings: **coma, comas**...<br>**asa, asas**... |
| ImpSub. | ALL | B4 | A–endings: **hablara**...<br>**comiera**...<br>OR **asiera**... |
| ImpSub. | ALL | B4, but change –**r** to –**s** | E–endings: **hablase**...<br>**comiese**...<br>**asiese**... |

| Present Participle | *–ar* verbs: | B1 base | **–ando**<br>**hablando** |
|---|---|---|---|
| | *–er/–ir* verbs: | B1 base | **–iendo**<br>**comiendo** |
| Past Participle | *–ar* verbs: | B1 base | **–ado**<br>**hablado** |
| | *–er/–ir* verbs: | B1 base | **–ido**<br>**comido** |

**Forms to use for Commands:** Use the present subjunctive for all commands *except* 2S and 2P positive forms.

Affirmative Commands:

| 1S | not used | 1P | 1P–present subj.<br>**¡Comamos!** |
|---|---|---|---|
| 2S | 3S–present<br>**¡Come!** | 2P | B1 base + **–ad, –ed,** or **–id**<br>**¡Hablad!**<br>**¡Comed!**<br>**¡Asid!** |
| 3S | 3S–present<br>subj.<br>**¡Coma!** | 3P | 3P–present subj.<br>**¡Coman!** |

Negative Commands:

| 1S | not used | 1P | 1P–present subj.<br>**¡No comamos!** |
|---|---|---|---|
| 2S | 2S–present subj.<br>**¡No comas!** | 2P | 2P–present subj.<br>**¡No comáis!** |
| 3S | 3S–present subj.<br>**¡No coma!** | 3P | 3P–present subj.<br>**¡No coman!** |

# Chapter 2

## Verb Irregularities I:
## Ten Spelling Rules

"I before E except after C." You probably learned this spelling rule in second grade. Almost as soon as you learned this rule you began running into its exceptions. Before long you likely wondered if the rule was really that useful after all.

All languages have spelling rules, and Spanish is no different. However, in Spanish there are *no exceptions* to the ten spelling rules outlined in this chapter. They apply to all Spanish verbs, even those often identified as "irregular." They also apply to words in other parts of speech.

These ten rules are easy to learn and understand, and once you have learned them, you will have no trouble recognizing when they are needed and applying them correctly. Because the rules are so consistently applied, it is hard to justify classifying verbs whose irregularity is only the result of a spelling rule as an irregular verb at all.

---

**These spelling rules have one major purpose: to preserve the integrity of the verb's sound as defined by its infinitive regardless of the verb's ending.**

---

The 1S-present subjunctive forms for the following four verbs have been purposefully misspelled. Carefully pronounce the infinitives and the proposed present subjunctives as shown.

| | | | |
|---|---|---|---|
| **buscar** | *to search for* | ⇨ | **busce**? |
| **cargar** | *to load, burden* | ⇨ | **carge**? |
| **vencer** | *to defeat* | ⇨ | **venca**? |
| **coger** | *to sieze, catch* | ⇨ | **coga**? |

Did you notice the changes in the sounds of these verbs? These examples illustrate the most common problem. It occurs when a verb that has a root or base ending in a "c" or "g" switches between using an A–ending and using an E–ending. Both "c" and "g" can have either a hard sound or a soft sound, depending on the vowel they precede. Consider:

A "c" before "a," "o," "u," or consonants has the *hard* sound, as in **contar** and **cantar**. But if it precedes an "e" or an "i" it has the *soft* sound, as in **cenar** and **hacienda**.

A "g" will have a *hard* sound before "a," "o," "u," or consonants, as in **gastar, gozar**, and **gustar**. But if it precedes an "e" or an "i" it takes on a *soft* sound as in **girar**. In English, this soft "g" is heard in *ginger*. However in Spanish, the soft "g" sounds like an English "h" or a Spanish "j."

For example, the word *garage* is spelled the same in both English and Spanish and illustrates both "g" sounds. In Spanish, the correct pronunciation is "gar-ah-hay."

Now try pronouncing the same four verbs shown above with their correct spellings for the 1S-present subjunctive forms, as shown below.

| | | | |
|---|---|---|---|
| **buscar** | *to search for* | ⇨ | **busque** |
| **cargar** | *to load, burden* | ⇨ | **cargue** |
| **vencer** | *to defeat* | ⇨ | **venza** |
| **coger** | *to sieze, catch* | ⇨ | **coja** |

The spelling rules provide substitutes for the "c" and "g" in these cases to preserve the sound of the infinitive throughout its conjugated forms.

These four cases, along with six others, constitute the ten spelling rules presented in this chapter. Rules R1 through R4 deal with –*ar* verbs, while rules R5 through R10 apply to –*er/–ir* verbs.

Since there are no exceptions to the spelling rules, only a representative sampling of verbs affected by each rule is presented. You will encounter hundreds of other verbs to which these rules apply. Knowing these simple rules and how to use them will help you to master each verb that you might encounter.

# Spelling Rule One – R1

**Infinitives ending in –car:** c ➪ qu

**Forms affected:** 1S–preterit and all of the present subjunctive.

| Pr |  |
|----|----|
|  |  |
|  |  |
|  |  |
| Im |  |
|  |  |
|  |  |
|  |  |
| Pret |  |
| 1S |  |

This change takes advantage of the **–que–** letter combination in which the "u" sound is silent, thus using **–qu–** to preserve the hard "c" sound of the infinitive when it would appear before an "e."

**ALL** verbs ending in –**car** conform to Spelling Rule **R1**, as illustrated below.

| F / C |  |
|----|----|
|  |  |
|  |  |
| P S |  |
| 1S | 1P |
| 2S | 2P |
| 3S | 3P |
| I S |  |
|  |  |
|  |  |

### Examples of R1 verbs

| Infinitive |  |  | 1S–preterit |
|----|----|----|----|
| buscar | *to search for* | ➪ | busqué |
| colocar | *to position* | ➪ | coloqué |
| fabricar | *to manufacture* | ➪ | fabriqué |
| identificar | *to identify* | ➪ | identifiqué |
| marcar | *to mark* | ➪ | marqué |
| platicar | *to chat* | ➪ | platiqué |
| secar | *to dry* | ➪ | sequé |
| tocar | *to touch* | ➪ | toqué |
| vivicar | *to enliven* | ➪ | viviqué |

**buscar**, *to search for*

Pres.Part: **buscando**   Past Part: **buscado**

| Pres: | | | Pret: | | | Fut: |
|----|----|----|----|----|----|----|
| busco | | | busqué | buscamos | | buscaré |
| Imp: | | | buscaste | buscasteis | | Cond: |
| buscaba | | | buscó | buscaron | | buscaría |

| Pres.Sub: | | Imp.Sub: |
|----|----|----|
| busque | busquemos | buscara |
| busques | busquéis | (buscase) |
| busque | busquen | |

# Spelling Rule Two – R2

**Infinitives ending in –gar:**  g ⇨ gu

**Forms affected:**  1S–preterit and all of the present subjunctive.

| | |
|---|---|
| Pr | |
| | |
| Im | |
| | |
| | |
| Pret | |
| 1S | |

This change takes advantage of the **–gue–** letter combination in which the "u" sound is silent, thus using **–gu–** to preserve the hard "g" sound of the infinitive when it would appear before an "e."

ALL verbs ending in **–gar** conform to Spelling Rule **R2**, as illustrated below.

### Examples of R2 verbs

| Infinitive | | | 1S–preterit |
|---|---|---|---|
| **agregar** | *to collect* | ⇨ | **agregué** |
| **cargar** | *to load* | ⇨ | **cargué** |
| **delegar** | *to delegate* | ⇨ | **delegué** |
| **fisgar** | *to snoop* | ⇨ | **fisgué** |
| **juzgar** | *to judge* | ⇨ | **juzgué** |
| **llegar** | *to arrive* | ⇨ | **llegué** |
| **negar** | *to deny* | ⇨ | **negué** |
| **pagar** | *to pay* | ⇨ | **pagué** |
| **regar** | *to sprinkle* | ⇨ | **regué** |

**agregar,** *to collect, gather, add, collate*

Pres.Part: **agregando**    Past Part: **agregado**

| Pres: agrego | Pret: agregué agregaste agregó | agregamos agregasteis agregaron | Fut: agregaré |
|---|---|---|---|
| Imp: agregaba | | | Cond: agregaría |
| Pres.Sub: agregue agregues agregue | agreguemos agreguéis agreguen | Imp.Sub: agregara (agregase) | |

# Spelling Rule Three – R3

**Infinitives ending in –zar:   z ⇨ c**

**Forms affected:** 1S–preterit and all of the present subjunctive.

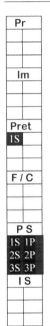

This change may have a historical basis. It is known that archaic Castilian vacillated between the spelling **gozar** and the Leonese/Portuguese spelling **goçar.** (Corominas and Pascual, *Diccionario Crítico Etimilógico Castellano e Hispánico* Vol. G-MA, page 185), which may account for the present-day z⇨c variations when the "z" would appear before an "e".

**ALL** verbs ending in –zar conform to Spelling Rule **R3**, as illustrated below.

### Examples of R3 verbs

| Infinitive | | | 1S–preterit |
|---|---|---|---|
| **abrazar** | *to hug, clasp* | ⇨ | **abracé** |
| **cruzar** | *to cross* | ⇨ | **crucé** |
| **danzar** | *to dance* | ⇨ | **dancé** |
| **organizar** | *to organize* | ⇨ | **organicé** |
| **sollozar** | *to sob* | ⇨ | **sollocé** |
| **utilizar** | *to use* | ⇨ | **utilicé** |

**gozar,** *to enjoy*

Pres.Part: **gozando**     Past Part: **gozado**

| Pres: | Pret: | | Fut: |
|---|---|---|---|
| **gozo** | **gocé** | **gozamos** | **gozaré** |
| Imp: | **gozaste** | **gozasteis** | Cond: |
| **gozaba** | **gozó** | **gozaron** | **gozaría** |

| Pres.Sub: | | Imp.Sub: |
|---|---|---|
| **goce** | **gocemos** | **gozara** |
| **goces** | **gocéis** | **(gozase)** |
| **goce** | **gocen** | |

# Spelling Rule Four – R4

**Infinitives ending in –guar:**  gu ⇨ gü

**Forms affected:**  1S–preterit and all of the present subjunctive.

| Pr |
|---|
|  |
|  |
| Im |
|  |
|  |
| Pret |
| 1S |

The distinct sound of the "u" in the –**guar** verbs would be lost in the –**gue**– letter combination if it were not for the dieresis over the "u" when it would appear before an "e".

**ALL** verbs ending in –**guar** conform to Spelling Rule **R4**, as illustrated below.

| F / C |
|---|
|  |
|  |
| P S |
| 1S 1P |
| 2S 2P |
| 3S 3P |
| I S |
|  |
|  |

**The six most common R4 verbs**

| Infinitive | | | 1S–preterit |
|---|---|---|---|
| aguar | *to dilute* | ⇨ | agüé |
| apaciguar | *to pacify* | ⇨ | apacigüé |
| averiguar | *to find out* | ⇨ | averigüé |
| fraguar | *to plot* | ⇨ | fragüé |
| menguar | *to diminish* | ⇨ | mengüé |
| santiguar | *to make the sign of the cross* | ⇨ | santigüé |

**averiguar,** *to find out, ascertain*

Pres.Part: **averiguando**      Past Part: **averiguado**

| Pres: averiguo | Pret: averigüé | averiguamos | Fut: averiguaré |
|---|---|---|---|
| Imp: averiguaba | averiguaste averiguó | averiguasteis averiguaron | Cond: averiguaría |

| Pres.Sub: | | Imp.Sub: |
|---|---|---|
| averigüe averigüemos | | averiguara |
| averigües averigüéis | | (averiguase) |
| averigüe averigüen | | |

# Spelling Rule Five – R5 & R5*

**Infinitives ending in –cer/–cir:  c ⇨ zc  or  c ⇨ z**

**Forms affected:** 1S–present and all of the present subjunctive.

One might wonder at the "sound preservation" principle with this one, but no one ever claimed that rules of language make perfect sense.

**Note: A few verbs ending in –cer/–cir have the c⇨z change. These exceptions will be denoted as R5\* and are listed on the following page.**

**ALL** verbs ending in **–cer** and **–cir** conform to Spelling Rule **R5 or R5\***, as illustrated below and on the following page.

### Examples of R5 verbs

| Infinitive | | | 1S-present |
|---|---|---|---|
| agradecer | *to thank* | ⇨ | agradezco |
| aparecer | *to appear* | ⇨ | aparezco |
| conocer | *to know* | ⇨ | conozco |
| crecer | *to grow* | ⇨ | crezco |
| merecer | *to deserve* | ⇨ | merezco |
| nacer | *to be born* | ⇨ | nazco |
| obedecer | *to obey* | ⇨ | obedezco |
| ofrecer | *to offer* | ⇨ | ofrezco |
| yacer | *to lie down* | ⇨ | yazco |

**nacer,** *to be born*

Pres.Part: **naciendo**   Past Part: **nacido**

| Pres: | | Pret: | Fut: |
|---|---|---|---|
| nazco | nacemos | nací | naceré |
| naces | nacéis | | |
| nace | nacen | | |
| Imp: | | | Cond: |
| nacía | | | nacería |
| Pres.Sub: | | Imp.Sub: | |
| nazca | nazcamos | naciera | |
| nazcas | nazcáis | (naciese) | |
| nazca | nazcan | | |

### The sixteen most common R5* verbs

| Infinitive | | | 1S–present |
|---|---|---|---|
| convencer | *to convince* | ⇨ | convenzo |
| disfruncir | *to unfurl* | ⇨ | disfrunzo |
| ejercer | *to exercize* | ⇨ | ejerzo |
| esparcir | *to scatter* | ⇨ | esparzo |
| estarcor | *to stencil* | ⇨ | estarzo |
| fruncir | *to furrow a brow* | ⇨ | frunzo |
| mecer | *to swing* | ⇨ | mezo |
| remecer | *to rock, swing* | ⇨ | remezo |
| resarcir | *to compensate* | ⇨ | resarzo |
| uncir | *to yoke* | ⇨ | unzo |
| vencer | *to conquer* | ⇨ | venzo |
| zurcir | *to darn* | ⇨ | zurzo |

**Cocer,** *to cook,* **recocer,** *to overcook,* **retorcer,** *to wring,* and **torcer,** *to twist,* are all R5* verbs. However, these verbs also exhibit V3 vowel variations and will be dealt with in Chapter 3.

**vencer,** *to conquer*

Pres.Part: **venciendo**  Past Part: **vencido**

| Pres: | | Pret: | Fut: |
|---|---|---|---|
| venzo | vencemos | vencí | venceré |
| vences | vencéis | | |
| vence | vencen | | |
| Imp: | | | Cond: |
| vencía | | | vencería |
| Pres.Sub: | | Imp.Sub: | |
| venza | venzamos | venciera | |
| venzas | venzáis | (venciese) | |
| venza | venzan | | |

# Spelling Rule Six – R6

**Infinitives ending in –ger/–gir:   g ⇨ j**

**Forms affected:** 1S–present and all of the present subjunctive.

| Pr |
|----|
| **1S** |
| Im |
| Pret |
| F / C |
| P S |
| IS 1P |
| 2S 2P |
| 3S 3P |
| I S |

This change allows the verb to maintain the soft "g" sound (similar to "h" in English) of the infinitive throughout its conjugation patterns, even when the ending is –**o** or begins with –**a**.

**ALL** verbs ending in –**ger** and –**gir**  conform to Spelling Rule **R6** as illustrated below.

### Examples of R6 verbs

| Infinitive | | | 1S–present |
|---|---|---|---|
| **dirigir** | *to direct* | ⇨ | **dirijo** |
| **emerger** | *to emerge* | ⇨ | **emerjo** |
| **fingir** | *to pretend* | ⇨ | **finjo** |
| **infligir** | *to inflict* | ⇨ | **inflijo** |
| **proteger** | *to protect* | ⇨ | **protejo** |
| **surgir** | *to spurt* | ⇨ | **surjo** |
| **urgir** | *to urge* | ⇨ | **urjo** |

**coger,** *to catch, seize, grab*
Pres.Part: **cogiendo**    Past Part: **cogido**

| Pres:  | | Pret: | Fut: |
|---|---|---|---|
| **cojo** | **cogemos** | **cogí** | **cogeré** |
| **coges** | **cogéis** | | |
| **coge** | **cogen** | | |
| Imp: | | | Cond: |
| **cogía** | | | **cogería** |
| Pres.Sub: | | Imp.Sub: | |
| **coja** | **cojamos** | **cogiera** | |
| **cojas** | **cojáis** | **(cogiese)** | |
| **coja** | **cojan** | | |

# Spelling Rule Seven – R7

**Infinitives ending in –guir:**  gu ⇨ g

**Forms affected:** 1S–present and all of the present subjunctive.

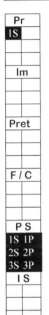

Since the "u" is not distinctly pronounced due to the –ui– diphthong in these verbs' infinitives, the "u" must be dropped before –o or before A–endings to preserve the silent "u" characteristic of the infinitive.

**ALL** verbs ending in –**guir** conform to Spelling Rule **R7** as illustrated below.

### The most common R7 verbs

| Infinitive | | | 1S–present |
|---|---|---|---|
| conseguir | *to obtain* | ⇨ | consigo |
| distinguir | *to distinguish* | ⇨ | distingo |
| erguir | *to raise* | ⇨ | yergo / irgo |
| extinguir | *to extinguish* | ⇨ | extingo |
| perseguir | *to pursue* | ⇨ | persigo |
| seguir | *to pursue* | ⇨ | sigo |
| subseguir | *to follow* | ⇨ | subsigo |

**distinguir,** *to distinguish*
Pres.Part: **distinguiendo**     Past Part: **distinguido**

| Pres: | | Pret: | Fut: |
|---|---|---|---|
| distingo | distinguimos | distinguí | distinguiré |
| distingues | distinguís | | |
| distingue | distinguen | | |
| Imp: | | | Cond: |
| distinguía | | | distinguiría |
| Pres.Sub: | | Imp.Sub: | |
| distinga | distingamos | distinguiera | |
| distingas | distingáis | (distinguiese) | |
| distinga | distingan | | |

# Spelling Rule Eight – R8

**Infinitives ending in –llir or –ñir:**
   **Drop the –i– in selected endings.**

**Forms affected:**    3S and 3P–preterit and all of the imperfect
                         subjunctive, and the present participle.

Note that the –ñ– and –ll– consonants have a "y-glide" sound built into them, so the *unaccented* –i– in endings such as **–ió, –ieron,** and **–iendo** that follow –ñ– and –ll– is unnecessary and must be eliminated from the spelling. Of course, only the *–er/–ir* verbs have these endings, and they appear in the 3S and 3P–preterit and also throughout the imperfect subjunctive (whose B4 base is based on the 3P–preterit). This change also affects the present participle for each of these *–er/–ir* verbs as well, whose normal present participle ending is **–iendo.**

**ALL** verbs ending in **–ñer, –ñir, –ller,** and **–llir** conform to Spelling Rule **R8** as illustrated below.

**Examples of R8 verbs**

| Infinitive | | | 3S–preterit | 3P–preterit |
|---|---|---|---|---|
| **bruñir** | *to polish* | ⇨ | **bruñó** | **bruñeron** |
| **bullir** | *to boil* | ⇨ | **bulló** | **bulleron** |
| **gruñir** | *to groan* | ⇨ | **gruñó** | **gruñeron** |
| **mullir** | *to fluff* | ⇨ | **mulló** | **mulleron** |
| **reñir** | *to quarrel* | ⇨ | **riñó** | **riñeron** |
| **tañer** | *to play (instr)* | ⇨ | **tañó** | **tañeron** |
| **teñir** | *to tint, dye* | ⇨ | **tiñó** | **tiñeron** |
| **uñir** | *to yoke* | ⇨ | **uñó** | **uñeron** |

## bullir, *to boil*

Pres.Part: **bullendo**     Past Part: **bullido**

| Pres: | Pret: | | Fut: |
|---|---|---|---|
| bullo | bullí | bullimos | bulliré |
| Imp: | bulliste | bullisteis | Cond: |
| bullía | bulló | bulleron | bulliría |

| Pres.Sub: | Imp.Sub: | |
|---|---|---|
| bulla | bullera | bulléramos |
| | bulleras | bullerais |
| | bullera | bulleran |
| | OR | |
| | bullese | bullésemos |
| | bulleses | bulleseis |
| | bullese | bullesen |

## tañer, *to pluck, play an instrument*

Pres.Part: **tañendo**     Past Part: **tañido**

| Pres: | Pret: | | Fut: |
|---|---|---|---|
| taño | tañí | tañimos | tañeré |
| Imp: | tañiste | tañisteis | Cond: |
| tañía | tañó | tañeron | tañería |

| Pres.Sub: | Imp.Sub: | |
|---|---|---|
| taña | tañera | tañéramos |
| | tañeras | tañerais |
| | tañera | tañeran |
| | OR | |
| | tañese | tañésemos |
| | tañeses | tañeseis |
| | tañese | tañesen |

# Spelling Rule Nine – R9 & R9*

*–er/–ir* verbs with a B1 base ending in –a, –e, or –o:
**Replace the –i– with a –y– in selected endings**
(e.g., for **raer**, the 3P–preterit is **rayeron**, not raieron).

*–er/–ir* verbs with a B1 base ending in –i– or –y–:
**Drop the –i– in selected endings**
(e.g., for **reir**, the 3P–preterit is **rieron**, not riieron).

**Forms affected:**
3S and 3P–preterit and all of the imperfect subjunctive, and the present participle.

| Pr |
|----|
| |
| |

| Im |
|----|
| |
| |

| Pret |
|------|

| 3S 3P |
|-------|
| F / C |
| |
| |

| P S |
|-----|
| |
| |
| I S |
| 1S 1P |
| 2S 2P |
| 3S 3P |

This change is made to avoid the following 3-vowel combinations with an "i" between two other vowels:

**R9: Substitute a –y–**

| aie ⇨ aye | eie ⇨ eye | oie ⇨ oye |
|-----------|-----------|-----------|
| aio ⇨ ayo | eio ⇨ eyo | oio ⇨ oyo |

**R9*: Remove an –i–**

| iie ⇨ ie | iio ⇨ io |
|----------|----------|

The inserted –y– provides a "y-glide" sound to connect the two vowels, which would not be obvious otherwise. In the case of the R9* spelling rule, some verbs display an e⇨i vowel variation (discussed in the following chapter), changing the B1 base. For these verbs, then, and ending beginning with –i– would result in a verb form with –ii–. (For example, **reir**'s B1 base is **ri**–and its 3P–preterit is **rieron**, not riieron.)

As with Rule 8, only *–er/–ir* verbs are affected, and the particular forms involved are the 3S– and 3P–preterit, all of the imperfect subjunctive, and the present participle.

ALL verbs having an –a–, –e–, or –o– before the –er or –ir ending in the infinitive conform to Spelling Rule **R9** as illustrated below.

### Examples of R9 verbs

| Infinitive | | | 3S–preterit | 3P–preterit |
|---|---|---|---|---|
| caer | *to fall* | ⇨ | cayó | cayeron |
| creer | *to believe* | ⇨ | creyó | creyeron |
| leer | *to read* | ⇨ | leyó | leyeron |
| oir | *to hear* | ⇨ | oyó | oyeron |
| raer | *to erase* | ⇨ | rayó | rayeron |
| roer | *to gnaw* | ⇨ | royó | royeron |

**leer,** *to read*

Pres.Part: **leyendo**     Past Part: **leido**

| Pres: | Pret: | | Fut: |
|---|---|---|---|
| leo | leí | leimos | leeré |
| Imp: | leiste | leisteis | Cond: |
| leía | leyó | leyeron | leería |

| Pres.Sub: | Imp.Sub: | |
|---|---|---|
| lea | leyera | leyéramos |
| | leyeras | leyerais |
| | leyera | leyeran |
| | OR | |
| | leyese | leyésemos |
| | leyeses | leyeseis |
| | leyese | leyesen |

# Spelling Rule Ten – R10

Two special cases: argüir and delinquir

| Pr |
|---|
| 1S |
| 2S |
| 3S 3P |
| Im |
| |
| |
| Pret |
| |
| |
| 3S 3P |
| F / C |
| |
| |
| P S |
| 1S 1P |
| 2S 2P |
| 3S 3P |
| I S |
| 1S 1P |
| 2S 2P |
| 3S 3P |

argüir

*–er/–ir* verbs ending in –güir:     gü ⇨ guy

**Forms affected:**
All of the present tense *except* 1P and 2P
3S and 3P–preterit
All of the present subjunctive
All of the imperfect subjunctive

The purpose for the dieresis over the –ü– in the infinitive is to keep the sound of the "u" even though it may appear in a –gui– letter combination. For –er/–ir verb forms that end in –o or have A–endings, the dieresis is unnecessary. (The –y– is added to ease the pronunciation shift between the –u– and a following –o or –a, an example of a V4 vowel variation dealt with in the following chapter.)

argüir is the only common verb that exhibits this.

**argüir,** *to argue*
    Pres.Part: **arguyendo**     Past Part: **argüido**

| Pres: | | Pret: | | Fut: |
|---|---|---|---|---|
| arguyo | argüimos | argüí | argüimos | argüiré |
| arguyes | argüís | argüiste | argüisteis | |
| arguye | arguyen | arguyó | arguyeron | Cond: |
| | | | | argüiría |
| Imp: **argüía** | | | | |

| Pres.Sub: | | Imp.Sub: | |
|---|---|---|---|
| arguya | arguyamos | arguyera | arguyéramos |
| arguyas | arguyáis | arguyeras | arguyeráis |
| arguya | arguyan | arguyera | arguyeran |
| | | OR | |
| | | arguyese | arguyésemos |
| | | arguyeses | arguyeséis |
| | | arguyese | arguyesen |

| Pr |
|----|
| 1S |
|    |
| Im |
|    |
|    |
| Pret |
|    |
| F / C |
|    |
|    |
| P S |
| 1S 1P |
| 2S 2P |
| 3S 3P |
| I S |
|    |
|    |

# delinquir

*–er/–ir* **verbs ending in –quir:**      qu ⇨ c

**Forms affected:**
   1S–present and all of the present subjunctive.

This change allows the verb to maintain the "k" sound and silent "u" produced by the –qui– diphthong in the infinitive throughout its conjugation patterns, even when the ending is an –o or begins with an –a–.

   There are only two common verbs that exhibit this variation.

| Infinitive | | 1S–present |
|---|---|---|
| **delinquir** *to violate the law* | ⇨ | **delinco** |
| **derrelinquir** *to abandon* | ⇨ | **derrelinco** |

**delinquir,** *to violate the law, be delinquent*
   Pres.Part: **delinquiendo**      Past Part: **delinquido**

| Pres: | | Pret: | Fut: |
|---|---|---|---|
| delinco  delinquimos | | delinquí | delinquiré |
| delinques  delinquís | | | |
| delinque  delinquen | | | |
| Imp: | | | Cond: |
| delinquía | | | delinquiría |
| Pres.Sub: | | Imp.Sub: | |
| delinca  delincamos | | delinquiera | |
| delincas  delincáis | | (delinquiese) | |
| delinca  delincan | | | |

# Summary of the Ten Spelling Rules

| *–ar* verbs<br>ending in: | (Forms affected: 1S–preterit<br>and all of present subjunctive) | |
|---|---|---|
| **R1**   **–car** | ⇨ | –c– changes to –**qu**– before "e" or "i"<br>**buscar** ⇨ **busqué** |
| **R2**   **–gar** | ⇨ | –g– changes to –**gu**– before "e" or "i"<br>**cargar** ⇨ **cargué** |
| **R3**   **–zar** | ⇨ | –z– changes to –**c**– before "e" or "i"<br>**alzar** ⇨ **alcé** |
| **R4**   **–guar** | ⇨ | –gu– changes to –**gü**– before "e" or "i"<br>**averiguar** ⇨ **averigüe** |

| *–er/–ir* verbs<br>ending in: | (Forms affected: 1s–present<br>and all of present subjunctive) | |
|---|---|---|
| **R5**   **–cer/–cir** | ⇨ | –c– changes to –**zc**– before "o" or "a"<br>**nacer** ⇨ **nazco** |
| **R5\***  **–cer/–cir** | ⇨ | –c–changes to –**z**– before "o" or "a"<br>**vencer** ⇨ **venzo** |
| **R6**   **–ger/–gir** | ⇨ | –g– changes to –**j**– before "o" or "a"<br>**coger** ⇨ **cojo** |
| **R7**   **–guer/–guir** | ⇨ | –gu– changes to –**g**– before "o" or "a"<br>**distinguir** ⇨ **distingo** |

| *–er/–ir* verbs with<br>base ending in –ñ–<br>or –ll– | (Forms affected: 3S, 3P–preterit,<br>imperfect subjunctive, and<br>present participle |
|---|---|

**R8**   Drop the –i– when it appears in the endings for the 3S– and 3P–preterit and throughout the imperfect subjunctive and in the present participle.

    **reñir** ⇨ **riñó, riñeron**      **bullir** ⇨ **bulló, bulleron**

| *–er/–ir* verbs with B1 base ending in –a–, –e–, or –o– | (Forms affected: 3S, 3P–preterit imperfect subjunctive, and the present participle |
|---|---|

**R9**    Replace the –i– with a –y– in endings for the 3S and 3P–preterit and throughout the imperfect subjunctive and in the present participle.

> **caer** ⇨ **cayó, cayeron**     **oir** ⇨ **oyó, oyeron**

**R9\***   Remove an –i– to avoid –ii– vowel combinations in 3S and 3P–preterit and throughout the imperfect subjunctive and in the present participle.

> **reir**    ⇨ **rió, rieron**

**R10**   **Two special cases:**

**argüir:**

> –güir ⇨ –gü– changes to –gu– before –o or –a–:
>
> > **argüir** ⇨ **arguyo**

**delinquir:**

> –quir ⇨ –qu– changes to –c– before –o or –a–:
>
> > **delinquir** ⇨ **delinco**

# Chapter 3

## Verb Irregularities II:
## Ten Vowel Variations

With the strict spelling rules out of the way, it is time to tackle another group of verbs that are commonly referred to as "irregular." These are the verbs in which a vowel in the last syllable of the base undergoes a significant change in some forms in selected tenses.

For example, base B1 for **contar,** *to count,* (**cont**–) becomes **cuent**– for the 1S, 2S, 3S, and 3P–present, and since the 1S–present is used to form base B3 for the present subjunctive, the **o**⇨**ue** change is carried over into the 1S, 2S, 3S and 3P–present subjunctive as well. Thus for these forms you have:

|     | Present   | Present Subjunctive |
|-----|-----------|---------------------|
| 1S  | cuento    | cuente              |
| 2S  | cuentas   | cuentes             |
| 3S  | cuenta    | cuente              |
| 3P  | cuentan   | cuenten             |

It is important to note, however, that these variations in base spellings don't always carry over into the 1P and 2P of the present or present subjunctive. For the example just cited, the 1P and 2P forms in *both* tenses (present and present subjunctive) remain unaffected by this variation. That is:

|     | Present   | Present Subjunctive |
|-----|-----------|---------------------|
| 1P  | contamos  | contemos            |
| 2P  | contáis   | contéis             |

You will find that this pattern holds true for Variations V2, V3 and V9 presented in this chapter.

Not all verbs with the requisite vowel structure (such as "o" in the last syllable of the root) undergo these changes. For example, the B1 bases for **robar,** *to steal,* and **comer,** *to eat,* **rob**– and **com**–, don't change at all. Thus as you learn individual verbs, you should also memorize which verbs incorporate these variations. If, when you learn the infinitive, you also learn the 1S and 3S forms in the present and the 3P–preterit, you will have gone a long way toward mastering verbs with the variations covered in this chapter. Those three forms will give you most of the information you need for correctly conjugating the verb in all of its seven simple tenses. For example,

| Infinitive: | contar | robar | caer |
|---|---|---|---|
| 1S–present: | cuento | robo | caigo |
| 3S–present: | cuenta | roba | cae |
| 3P–preterit: | contaron | robaron | cayeron |

---

Some verbs exhibit more than one variation throughout their conjugations, and the inevitable spelling rules covered in the previous chapter are always in effect. Thus memorization and practice are still the only recourse for gaining mastery over Spanish irregular verbs.

---

For each variation presented in this chapter, a conjugation diagram and table like those used in the previous chapter are shown, highlighting the particular forms that are affected by that variation. In chapter two only a few sample verbs were given for each spelling rule. In this chapter and the next, we have tried to list *all* of the commonly encountered verbs that are affected by each variation. You will find that these lists provide a useful and easy reference to verbs that exhibit vowel-variation irregularities.

Many of the Truly Irregular Verbs also incorporate one or more of these variations (while following the spelling rules as well). Most of these verbs have verb families whose members contain the parent verb. For example, **tener** is the parent verb for a verb family that includes **detener**, **obtener**, **mantener**, and others. These verbs and their family members have been omitted from the verb lists in this chapter as they are dealt with in detail in Chapter 4.

# Variation One – V1 & V1*

| Consonant added to 1S–present: | V1: | insert –g– |
| | V1*: | insert –ig– |

**Forms affected:**
1S–present and all of the present subjunctive tense

| Pr |
|----|
| 1S |
| |
| Im |
| |
| Pret |
| |
| F / C |
| |
| P S |
| 1S 1P |
| 2S 2P |
| 3S 3P |
| I S |
| |

When *any* variation occurs in the 1S–present, that change trumps ALL other variations that may otherwise have affected the present subjunctive tense.

### V1  The most common verbs that insert –g–

| Infinitive | | | 1S–present | 1S–present subjunctive |
|------------|--|--|------------|------------------------|
| asir | *to sieze* | ⇨ | asgo | asga |
| desasir | *to release* | ⇨ | desasgo | desasga |
| equivaler | *to equal* | ⇨ | equivalgo | equivalga |
| prevaler | *to prevail* | ⇨ | prevalgo | prevalga |
| resalir | *to jut out* | ⇨ | resalgo | resalga |
| salir | *to leave* | ⇨ | salgo | salga |
| sobresalir | *to excel* | ⇨ | sobresalgo | sobresalga |
| valer | *to be worth* | ⇨ | valgo | valga |

### V1*  The most common verbs that insert –ig–

| Infinitive | | | 1S–present | 1S–present subjunctive |
|------------|--|--|------------|------------------------|
| caer | *to fall* | ⇨ | caigo | caiga |
| decaer | *to decline* | ⇨ | decaigo | decaiga |
| desoir | *to ignore* | ⇨ | desoigo | desoiga |
| oir | *to hear* | ⇨ | oigo | oiga |
| raer | *to erase* | ⇨ | raigo | raiga |
| raerse | *to wear away* | ⇨ | me raigo | me raiga |
| recaer | *to relapse* | ⇨ | recaigo | recaiga |
| roer | *to gnaw* | ⇨ | roigo | roiga |

**asir,** *to grasp, seize* **V1**

Pres.Part: **asiendo**      Past Part: **asido**

| Pres: | | Pret: | Fut: |
|---|---|---|---|
| asgo | asimos | así | asiré |
| ases | asís | | |
| ase | asen | | |
| Imp: | | | Cond: |
| asía | | | asiría |
| Pres.Sub: | | Imp.Sub: | |
| asga | asgamos | asiera | |
| asgas | asgáis | (asiese) | |
| asga | asgan | | |

Note that **asir, salir,** and **valer** verb families account for all of the V1 variation verbs, and that **caer, oir,** and **raer** verb families account for most of the V1* verbs.

The conjugation chart for **oír,** *to hear,* is shown below. **Oír** clearly shows that a V1 or V1* variation takes precedence over other changes in the present subjunctive. **Oír** also belongs to the group of V4 variation verbs, which exhibit the insertion of a –**y**– in various forms, as illustrated below. Normally, V4 would dictate that this –**y**– insertion also take place in the present subjunctive. But for **oír,** the V1* variation overrides this, so there are no –**y**– changes in the present subjunctive. Note also the unusual accent pattern in **oír**'s conjugation.

**oír,** *to hear*      **R9, V1, V4**

Pres.Part: **oyendo**      Past Part: **oido**

| Pres: | | Pret: | | Fut: |
|---|---|---|---|---|
| oigo | oímos | oí | oímos | oiré |
| oyes | oís | oíste | oísteis | |
| oye | oyen | oyó | oyeron | |
| Imp: | | | | Cond: |
| oía | | | | oiría |
| Pres.Sub: | | Imp.Sub: | | |
| oiga | oigamos | oyera | | |
| oigas | oigáis | (oyese) | | |
| oiga | oigan | | | |

# Variation Two – V2

**B1 and B3 base vowel change:**     e ⇨ ie

**Forms affected:**

All of the present tense *except* 1P & 2P
All of the present subjunctive tense *except* 1P & 2P

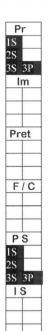

Note that the 1P and 2P forms in *both* affected tenses remain unchanged. This is one of the most common verb variations.

Several verbs show both this variation and an e⇨i variation as well. These verbs are dealt with under Variation V6.

**Errar**, *to err,* exhibits a slight twist on this variation, since the "e" to be replaced is the first letter in the word. In this case, it is replaced with **ye–** instead of **ie–**, leading to **yerro,** for the 1S–present  The rest of the V2 pattern follows this lead, as shown in the table on the following page.

This behavior is also seen with **erguir**, *to raise, to lift,* as an alternate form. That is, you may encounter **erguir** in the present and present subjunctive tenses with an added "y" or without.

**Examples of Verbs that exhibit the V2 variation**

| Infinitive | | | 1S–present | 1S–present subjunctive |
|---|---|---|---|---|
| calentar | *to warm* | ⇨ | caliento | caliente |
| cerrar | *to close* | ⇨ | cierro | cierre |
| defender | *to defend* | ⇨ | defiendo | defienda |
| despertar | *to awaken* | ⇨ | despierto | despierte |
| gobernar | *to govern* | ⇨ | gobierno | gobierne |
| helar | *to freeze* | ⇨ | hielo | hiele |
| sentar | *to seat, sit* | ⇨ | siento | siente |

## cerrar, *to close*

Pres.Participle: **cerrando**     Past Part: **cerrado**

| Pres: | | Pret: | Fut: |
|---|---|---|---|
| cierro | cerramos | cerré | cerraré |
| cierras | cerráis | | |
| cierra | cierran | | |
| Imp: | | | Cond: |
| cerraba | | | cerraría |
| Pres.Sub: | | Imp.Sub: | |
| cierre | cerremos | cerrara | |
| cierres | cerréis | (cerrase) | |
| cierre | cierren | | |

## errar, *to err*

Pres.Participle: **errando**     Past Part: **errado**

| Pres: | | Pret: | Fut: |
|---|---|---|---|
| yerro | erramos | erré | erraré |
| yerras | erráis | | |
| yerra | yerran | | |
| Imp: | | | Cond: |
| erraba | | | erraría |
| Pres.Sub: | | Imp.Sub: | |
| yerre | erremos | errara | |
| yerres | erréis | (errase) | |
| yerre | yerren | | |

## The most common verbs that exhibit the V2 variation:

| | | | |
|---|---|---|---|
| abnegar | *to forego* | encender | *to incite, inflame* |
| acertar | *to guess right* | encentar | *to begin* |
| alentar | *to breath, inspire* | encerrar | *to enclose* |
| apretar | *to grip, press* | encerrarse | *to be locked up* |
| arrendar | *to lease, rent* | encomendar | *to commend* |
| asentar | *to seat, set down* | endentar | *to engage, mesh* |
| atender | *to attend to* | enhestar | *to lift, raise* |
| atravesar | *to cross* | enmelar | *to smear with* |
| calentar | *to heat up* | | *honey* |
| cegar | *to blind* | enmendar | *to amend, revise* |
| cerrar | *to close* | entender | *to understand* |
| comenzar | *to begin, start* | enterrar | *to bury, forget* |
| concernir | *to be pertinent to* | entesar | *to tighten, stretch* |
| concertar | *to arrange, agree* | entrecerrar | *to leave ajar* |
| condescender | *to comply* | erguir | *to raise* |
| confesar | *to confess, admit* | erguirse | *to stiffen* |
| defender | *to defend* | errar | *to err, miss* |
| denegar | *to deny; to refuse* | escarmentar | *to chastise* |
| dentar | *to teeth, serrate* | extender | *to extend* |
| desacertar | *to be wrong, err* | fregar | *to scrub* |
| desalentar | *to make breathless* | hacendar | *to transfer* |
| desatender | *to neglect* | | *property to* |
| descender | *to descend* | heder | *to stink, reek* |
| desconcertar | *to disconcert* | helar | *to freeze* |
| desdentar | *to extract (teeth)* | hender | *to split, crack* |
| desenterrar | *to unearth, dig up* | herrar | *to shoe a horse* |
| desgobernar | *to misgovern* | invernar | *to spend the winter* |
| deshelar | *to thaw* | manifestar | *to manifest, show* |
| desherrar | *to unshackle* | mentar | *to mention* |
| desmedirse | *to forget oneself* | merendar | *to have a snack* |
| despertar | *to wake someone* | negar | *to deny; to forbid* |
| desplegar | *to unfold, unfurl* | nevar | *to snow* |
| desterrar | *to banish, exile* | pensar | *to think, believe* |
| discernir | *to discern* | perder | *to lose, squander* |
| distender | *to distend, stretch* | plegar | *to fold, crease* |
| emparentar | *to marry into* | plegarse | *to bend ,submit* |
| empedernir | *to harden* | quebrar | *to break, smash* |
| empedrar | *to pave* | recalentar | *to reheat* |
| empezar | *to begin, start* | recomendar | *to recommend* |

## V2 Variation Verbs (cont.)

| | | | |
|---|---|---|---|
| refregar | *to rub, scrub* | sosegar | *to quiet, calm* |
| regar | *to water, irrigate* | soterrar | *to burry, hide* |
| regimentar | *to regiment* | subarrendar | *to sublet* |
| remendar | *to mend* | subentender | *to grasp, infer* |
| renegar | *to abhor, deny strongly* | temblar | *to tremble, shake* |
| | | tender | *to spread out;* |
| repetir | *to repeat* | tentar | *to feel, touch to try, attempt* |
| reventar | *to burst, explode* | | |
| reverter | *to overflow* | transcender | *to transcend* |
| salpimentar | *to season* | trascender | *to smell* |
| segar | *to cut, mow* | trasegar | *to decant; to upset, overturn* |
| sembrar | *to sow,seed* | | |
| sementar | *to seed, sow* | trasverter | *to overflow* |
| sentar (-se) | *to seat, (sit down); to establish* | tropezar | *to stumble, blunder* |
| | | verter | *to pour, empty, spill; to translate* |
| serrar | *to saw* | | |
| sobrentender | *to infer, understand* | | |

# Variation Three – V3

---

**B1 and B3 base vowel change:**     o ⇨ ue

**Forms affected:**
All of the present tense *except* 1P & 2P
All of the present subjunctive tense *except* 1P & 2P

---

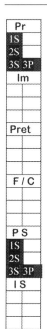

Note that the 1P and 2P forms in *both* affected tenses remain unchanged. Like variation V2, this variation is quite common.

In Variation V3 verbs, if a "g" precedes the –o– that changes to –ue–, spelling rule R4 (**gue**⇨**güe**) is observed as well to preserve the distinct sound of the "u" (e.g., **agorar** *to foretell* ⇨ **agüero**).

A special note is needed for the verbs **oler**, *to smell*, and **desosar**, *to bone, to pit*, which exhibit a V3 variation. In addition to the o⇨ue changes shown above, an initial **h**– is added wherever the V3 change takes place. Thus the 1S-present for these verbs becomes **huelo** and **deshueso**. As usual, the 1P and 2P forms are unaffected, giving **olemos** and **oléis** in the present and **olamos** and **oláis** in the present subjunctive for **oler**. **Desosar** is conjugated similarly. (Interestingly, **osar**, *to dare*, does not exhibit this behavior and has a perfectly regular conjugation.)

**Examples of Verbs that exhibit the V3 Variation**

| Infinitive | | | 1S–present | 1S–present subjunctive |
|---|---|---|---|---|
| **acordar** | *to agree* | ⇨ | **acuerdo** | **acuerde** |
| **contar** | *to count* | ⇨ | **cuento** | **cuente** |
| **costar** | *to cost* | ⇨ | **cuesto** | **cueste** |
| **forzar** | *to force* | ⇨ | **fuerzo** | **fuerce** *(R3)* |
| **mover** | *to move* | ⇨ | **muevo** | **mueva** |
| **rogar** | *to beg* | ⇨ | **ruego** | **ruegue** *(R2)* |

**contar,** *to count, relate, tell*

Pres.Part: **contando**     Past Part: **contado**

| Pres: | | Pret: | Fut: |
|---|---|---|---|
| cuento | contamos | conté | contaré |
| cuentas | contáis | | |
| cuenta | cuentan | | |
| Imp: | | | Cond: |
| contaba | | | contaría |
| Pres.Sub: | | Imp.Sub: | |
| cuente | contemos | contara | |
| cuentes | contéis | (contase) | |
| cuente | cuenten | | |

**oler,** *to smell*

Pres.Part: **oliendo**     Past Part: **olido**

| Pres: | | Pret: | Fut: |
|---|---|---|---|
| huelo | olemos | olí | oleré |
| hueles | oléis | | |
| huele | huelen | | |
| Imp: | | | Cond: |
| olía | | | olería |
| Pres.Sub: | | Imp.Sub: | |
| huela | olamos | oliera | |
| huelas | oláis | (oliese) | |
| huela | huelan | | |

## The most common verbs that exhibit the V3 variation

| | |
|---|---|
| **absolver** | *to absolve, acquit* |
| **acordar** | *to agree (upon)* |
| **acordarse** | *to remember* |
| **acostar** | *to put to bed* |
| **acostarse** | *to go to bed* |
| **almorzar** | *to have lunch* |
| **apostar** | *to bet, wager* |
| **aprobar** | *to prove, pass test* |
| **cocer** | *to cook* |
| **colar** | *to filter, strain* |
| **colgar** | *to hang up* |
| **comprobar** | *to verify, prove* |
| **conmover** | *to move emotionally* |
| **consolar** | *to console* |
| **contar** | *to count; to relate, tell* |
| **costar** | *to cost* |
| **degollar** | *to decapitate* |
| **demoler** | *to demolish, destroy* |
| **demostrar** | *to demonstrate* |
| **desacordar** | *to put in discord* |
| **desacordarse** | *to become forgetful* |
| **desaprobar** | *to disapprove, condemn* |
| **descolgar** | *to take down* |
| **descollar** | *to excell, stand out* |
| **desconsolar** | *to distress, grieve* |
| **descontar** | *to discount, deduct* |
| **desenvolver** | *to unwrap* |
| **desolar** | *to ravage* |
| **desollar** | *to skin, flay* |
| **desosar** | *to bone, pit* |
| **despoblar** | *to depopulate* |
| **devolver** | *to return, refund* |
| **discordar** | *to differ, disagree* |
| **disolver** | *to disolve* |
| **doler** | *to ache, hurt* |
| **emporcar** | *to soil, dirty* |
| **encontrar** | *to meet, encounter* |
| **encordar** | *to string (an instrument)* |
| **engrosar** | *to thicken* |

| | |
|---|---|
| **ensolver** | *to include, reduce, condense* |
| **entortar** | *to make cooked* |
| **envolver** | *to wrap up* |
| **envolverse** | *to have an affair, become involved* |
| **esforzar** | *to strengthen, encourage* |
| **esforzarse** | *to make an effort* |
| **forzar** | *to force; to rape* |
| **holgar** | *to rest, loaf* |
| **holgarse** | *to have a good time, relax* |
| **hollar** | *to tread upon, trample* |
| **llover** | *to rain* |
| **moblar** | *to furnish* |
| **moler** | *to mill, grind* |
| **morder (-se)** | *to bite, gnaw* |
| **mostrar** | *to show, demonstrate* |
| **mover** | *to move; persuade* |
| **oler** | *to smell, scent* |
| **poblar** | *to populate, colonize* |
| **probar** | *to test, prove, try on* |
| **promover** | *to promote, advance* |
| **recocer** | *to overcook* |
| **recontar** | *to recount* |
| **recordar** | *to remember, recall* |
| **recostar** | *to lean on; to lean* |
| **reforzar** | *to reinforce* |
| **regoldar** | *to belch, burp* |
| **remorder** | *to bite, gnaw* |
| **remover** | *to remove, take away* |
| **remover** | *to transfer, remove* |
| **renovar** | *to renew* |
| **repoblar** | *to repopulate* |
| **reprobar** | *to reprove* |
| **resolver** | *to resolve a problem* |
| **resonar** | *to resonate, echo* |
| **retorcer** | *to wring, twist* |
| **retostar** | *to toast brown* |

## V3 Variation Verbs (cont.)

| | | | |
|---|---|---|---|
| revolcar | *to knock down* | tostarse | *to become sunburned* |
| revolver | *to mix, stir, turn over* | trascolar | *to strain, filter* |
| rodar | *to roll, revolve* | trascolarse | *to percolate* |
| rogar | *to beg, pray, ask for* | trastrocar | *to rearrange, change* |
| solar | *to pave, tile* | trasvolar | *to fly over* |
| soldar | *to solder, weld* | trocar | *to exchange* |
| soler | *to be accustomed to* | tronar | *to thunder* |
| soltar | *to loosen, untie* | volar | *to fly; explode* |
| sonar | *to ring, echo, sound* | volcar | *to overturn, capsize* |
| soñar | *to dream* | | |
| torcer | *to twist, wind* | | |
| tostar | *to toast, tan* | | |

# Variation Four – V4

**B1, B3 and B4 base change:**      insert –y–
(All verbs in this group end in –**uir** *except* **oir** and **desoir.**)

**Forms affected:**
     All of the present tense *except* 1P & 2P
     3S and 3P in the preterit tense
     All of the present subjunctive tense
     All of the imperfect subjunctive tense
     The present participle

Unlike variations V2 and V3, only the 1P and 2P–present forms remain unchanged in variation V4. All six of the present subjunctive forms are affected.

     Note that this variation places a –**y**– directly in front of the pI–endings in the 3S and 3P–preterit and in the imperfect subjunctive. This situation invokes spelling rule R9*, causing the letter "i" in these endings to be dropped.

     A special note is necessary for the verbs **oir** *to hear* and **desoir** *to ignore*. These two verbs have a V1* variation in which an –**ig**– is inserted in the 1S–present (which dictates the B3 base for the present subjunctive), giving **oigo** and **desoigo**. Because a V1* variation trumps all others in the present subjunctive when it occurs, the present subjunctive for these two verbs reflects the V1* changes, not the V4 changes. The conjugation chart for **oir** is shown in detail under the variation V1 heading.

**Examples of Verbs that exhibit the V4 Variation**

| Infinitive | | | 1S-present | 3P-preterit |
|---|---|---|---|---|
| **argüir** | *to argue* | ⇨ | **arguyo** | **arguyeron** |
| **concluir** | *to conclude* | ⇨ | **concluyo** | **concluyeron** |
| **huir** | *to escape, flee* | ⇨ | **huyo** | **huyeron** |

**huir,**  *to escape, flee, run away*

Pres.Part: **huyendo**    Past Part: **huido**

| Pres: | | Pret: | | Fut: |
|---|---|---|---|---|
| huyo | huimos | huí | huimos | huiré |
| huyes | huís | huiste | huisteis | |
| huye | huyen | huyó | huyeron | |
| Imp: | | | | Cond: |
| huía | | | | huiría |

| Pres.Sub: | | Imp.Sub: | |
|---|---|---|---|
| huya | huyamos | huyera | huyéramos |
| huya | huyáis | huyeras | huyerais |
| huya | huyan | huyera | huyeran |
| | | or | |
| | | huyese | huyésemos |
| | | huyeses | huyeseis |
| | | huyese | huyesen |

**The most common verbs that exhibit the V4 variation**

| afluir | *to flow* | huir | *to escape, fle* |
|---|---|---|---|
| argüir | *to argue, infer* | imbuir | *to instill; imbue* |
| atribuir | *to attribute* | incluir | *to include* |
| concluir | *to conclude, finish* | influir | *to influence* |
| confluir | *to converge, join* | inmiscuir | *to mix* |
| constituir | *to constitute, make up* | instituir | *to institute* |
| construir | *to contract, build* | instruir | *to instruct, teach* |
| contribuir | *to contribute, pay* | intuir | *to sense* |
| desoir | *to ignore* | luir | *to rub* |
| destituir | *to dismiss, deprive* | obstruir | *to obstruct* |
| destruir | *to destroy* | ocluir | *to occlude* |
| diluir | *to dissolve; to dilute* | oir | *to hear, listen* |
| diminuir | *to diminish, lessen* | prostituir | *to prostitute* |
| distribuir | *to distribute* | recluir | *to shut in, seclude* |
| estatuir | *to establish, enact* | reconstruir | *to rebuild, reconstruct* |
| excluir | *to exclude* | rehuir | *refuse, avoid, shun* |
| fluir | *to flow* | restituir | *to refund, give back* |
| fruir | *to enjoy ones* | retribuir | *to repay, reward* |
| | *accomplishments* | substituir | *to substitute, replace* |

# Variation Five – V5

**B1, B3 and B4 base vowel change:    e ⇨ i**
(Only *–ir* verbs are affected by this change.)

**Forms affected:**
       All of the present tense *except* 1P & 2P
       3S and 3P in the preterit tense
       All of the present subjunctive tense
       All of the imperfect subjunctive tense
       The present participle

| Pr |
|---|
| 1S |
| 2S |
| 3S 3P |
| **Im** |
| |
| |
| **Pret** |
| |
| |
| 3S 3P |
| **F / C** |
| |
| |
| **P S** |
| 1S 1P |
| 2S 2P |
| 3S 3P |
| I S |
| 1S 1P |
| 2S 2P |
| 3S 3P |

Unlike variations V2 and V3, only the 1P and 2P forms in the present tense remain unchanged in variation V5. All six of the present subjunctive forms are affected.

    **Erguir,** *to raise,* has two different conjugations. The first uses this V5 variation pattern, in which the initial **e–** is replaced with **i–**, giving **irgo**, for example. The alternative conjugation is more properly described as a V6 variation and is explained more fully in the next section.

### Examples of Verbs that exhibit the V5 Variation

| Infinitive | | | 1S-present | 3P-preterit |
|---|---|---|---|---|
| colegir | *to collect* | ⇨ | colijo | colijieron*(R6)* |
| elegir | *to elect* | ⇨ | elijo | elijieron *(R6)* |
| freir | *to fry* | ⇨ | frío | frieron |
| gemir | *to moan* | ⇨ | gimo | gimieron |
| impedir | *to obstruct* | ⇨ | impido | impidieron |
| medir | *to measure* | ⇨ | mido | midieron |
| reir | *to laugh* | ⇨ | río | rieron |
| reñir | *to quarrel* | ⇨ | riño | riñeron *(R10)* |
| seguir | *to follow* | ⇨ | sigo | siguieron |
| teñir | *to dye, tint* | ⇨ | tiño | tiñeron *(R10)* |
| vestir | *to dress* | ⇨ | visto | vistieron |

**pedir,** *to ask for, request*

Pres.Part: **pidiendo**     Past Part: **pedido**

| Pres: | | Pret: | | Fut: |
|---|---|---|---|---|
| pido | pedimos | pedí | pedimos | pediré |
| pides | pedís | pediste | pedisteis | |
| pide | piden | pidió | pidieron | |
| **Imp:** | | | | **Cond:** |
| **pedía** | | | | **pediría** |

| Pres.Sub: | | Imp.Sub: | |
|---|---|---|---|
| pida | pidamos | pidiera | pidiéramos |
| pidas | pidáis | pidieras | pidierais |
| pida | pidan | pidiera | pidieran |
| | | or | |
| | | pidiese | pidiésemos |
| | | pidieses | pidieseis |
| | | pidiese | pidiesen |

## The most common verbs that exhibit the V5 variation

| colegir | *to collect* | investir | *to invest* |
|---|---|---|---|
| competir | *to compete, contest* | medir | *to measure* |
| concebir | *to conceive, imagine* | pedir | *to ask for, beg* |
| conseguir | *to get, obtain, attain* | perseguir | *to pursue, persecute* |
| corregir | *to correct, amend* | preconcebir | *to preconceive* |
| derretir | *to liquify, melt, thaw* | proseguir | *to continue, follow* |
| desleír | *to dissolve* | reelegir | *to reelect* |
| despedir | *to dismiss, fire* | refreir | *to refry* |
| despedirse | *to say good-bye to* | regir | *to govern, rule* |
| desteñir | *to fade* | reír | *to laugh* |
| desvestirse | *to undress* | rendir | *to defeat, overthrow* |
| elegir | *to elect, select, choose* | reñir | *to scold, quarrel* |
| embestir | *to attack, charge* | repetir | *to repeat* |
| engreir | *to spoil, pamper* | seguir | *to follow, continue* |
| erguir | *to raise* | servir | *to serve* |
| estreñir | *to constipate* | sofreir | *to fry lightly* |
| expedir | *to expedite* | sonreir | *to smile* |
| freir | *to fry* | subseguir | *to follow, come after* |
| gemir | *to moan* | teñir | *to dye, tint* |
| henchir | *to fill, stuff* | transgredir | *to transgress* |
| heñir | *to knead dough* | vestir | *to clothe, dress; wear* |
| impedir | *to impede, hinder* | | |

# Variation Six – V6

---

**BOTH of the following changes occur:**

**B1 and B3 base vowels changes:**     e ⇨ ie
**B3 and B4 base vowel change:**      e ⇨ i

(Only *–ir* verbs are affected by these changes.)

**Forms affected:**
    e ⇨ ie
       All of the present tense *except* 1P & 2P
       All of the present subjunctive tense *except* 1P & 2P
    e ⇨ i
       3S and 3P in the preterit tense
       1P and 2P of the present subjunctive tense
       All of the imperfect subjunctive tense
       The present participle

---

Some verbs subscribe to both the V2 variation and the V5 variation. The diagrams on the following page show what happens when the V2 variation is overlayed onto the V5 variation, resulting in the V6 variation outlined in this section.

In this situation, the V2 variation (gray cells) trumps the V5 variation (black cells), so wherever a conflict might arise, the V2 wins. Thus all of the forms normally affected by the V2 variation in both the present and the present subjunctive show the V2 e⇨ie change. However, the 1P and 2P–present subjunctive, which are unaffected by the V2 influence, show the underlying affect of the V5 variation.

The V5 variation still controls the 3S and 3P–preterit forms, all of the imperfect subjunctive, and the present participle.

**Venir** exhibits both an **e⇨ie** and e⇨i variation, but it is categorized as one of the Truly Irregular Verbs and will be dealt with in the next chapter.

| V2 | V5 | V6 |
|----|----|----|

Erguir, *to raise,* is actually a V5 variation verb, with the **e–** being replaced by **i–** in the appropriate forms, as described in the previous section. However, there is also a second alternative conjugation pattern for **erguir,** in which the initial **e–** is replaced with **ye–** in the present and present subjunctive tenses, just like **errar** (see Variation V2). This combination of V2 and V5 characteristics places this alternative conjugation for **erguir** in the V6 category.

There is also one uncharacteristic element for **erguir**. In this alternative conjugation, the 1P and 2P–present subjunctive forms for **erguir** also exhibit the **e⇨ye** pattern, unlike any other V2 verb. The resulting conjugation chart for **erguir** is shown on the next page.

**Examples of Verbs that exhibit the V6 variation**

| Infinitive | | | 1S–present | 3P–preterit |
|------------|--|--|------------|-------------|
| **advertir** | *to notice* | ⇨ | **advierto** | **advirtieron** |
| **preferir** | *to prefer* | ⇨ | **prefiero** | **prefirieron** |
| **requerir** | *to require* | ⇨ | **requiero** | **requirieron** |
| **sentir** | *to feel* | ⇨ | siento | sintieron |

## mentir   *to lie, tell a lie*

Pres.Part: **mintiendo**        Past Part: **mentido**

| Pres: | | Pret: | | Fut: |
|---|---|---|---|---|
| miento | mentimos | mentí | mentimos | **mentiré** |
| mientes | mentís | mentiste | mentisteis | |
| miente | mienten | mintió | mintieron | |
| **Imp:** | | | | **Cond:** |
| **mentía** | | | | **mentiría** |
| Pres.Sub: | | Imp.Sub: | | |
| mienta | mintamos | mintiera | mintiéramos | |
| mientas | mintáis | mintieras | mintiereis | |
| mienta | mientan | mintiera | mintieran | |
| | | or | | |
| | | mintiese | mintiésemos | |
| | | mintieses | mintieseis | |
| | | mintiese | mintiesen | |

## erguir,   *to raise*   (alternative conjugation)

Pres.Part: **irguiendo**        Past Part: **erguido**

| Pres: | | Pret: | | Fut: |
|---|---|---|---|---|
| yergo | erguimos | **erguí** | **erguimos** | **erguiré** |
| yergues | erguís | **erguiste** | **erguisteis** | |
| yergue | yerguen | irguió | irguieron | |
| **Imp:** | | | | **Cond:** |
| **erguía** | | | | **erguiría** |
| Pres.Sub: | | Imp.Sub: | | |
| yerga | yergamos | irguiera | irguiéramos | |
| yergas | yergáis | irguieras | irguiereis | |
| yerga | yergan | irguiera | irguieran | |
| | | or | | |
| | | irguiese | irguiésemos | |
| | | irguieses | irguieseis | |
| | | irguiese | irguiesen | |

## The most common verbs that exhibit the V6 variation

| | | | |
|---|---|---|---|
| **advertir** | *to advise; to warn* | **injerir** | *to inject, insert* |
| **asentir** | *to assent, agree* | **interferir** | *to interfere* |
| **conferir** | *to confer, compare* | **invertir** | *to invert, reverse* |
| **consentir** | *to consent, allow* | **malherir** | *to injure, wound* |
| **convertir** | *to convert; to change* | **mentir** | *to lie* |
| **deferir** | *to defer; to delegate* | **pervertir** | *to pervert, corrupt* |
| **desmentir** | *to contradict, disprove* | **preferir** | *to prefer* |
| | | **presentir** | *to have a hunch* |
| **diferir** | *to differ, defer, delay* | **proferir** | *to utter, speak* |
| **digerir** | *to digest* | **referir** | *to refer, relate* |
| **disentir** | *to dissent, differ* | **requerir** | *to require* |
| **divertir** | *to amuse, entertain* | **revertir** | *to revert* |
| **divertirse** | *to enjoy oneself* | **sentir** | *to feel, feel regret* |
| **erguir** | *to raise* | **sentirse** | *to feel (well, ill)* |
| **erguirse** | *to swell with pride* | **subvertir** | *to subvert, disturb* |
| **herir** | *to wound, injure* | **sugerir** | *to hint, suggest* |
| **hervir** | *to boil* | **transferir** | *to transfer* |
| **inferir** | *to infer, imply* | **zaherir** | *to censure, reprove* |
| **ingerir** | *to ingest* | | |

# Variation Seven – V7

**BOTH of the following changes occur:**

**B1 and B3 base vowels changes:**     o ⇨ ue
**B3 and B4 base vowel change:**     o ⇨ u

**Forms affected:**

o ⇨ ue
> All of the present tense *except* 1P & 2P
> All of the present subjunctive tense *except* 1P & 2P

o ⇨ u
> 3S and 3P in the preterit tense
> 1P and 2P of the present subjunctive tense
> ALL of the imperfect subjunctive tense
> The present participle

| Pr | |
|----|----|
| 1S | |
| 2S | |
| 3S | 3P |
| Im | |
| | |
| | |
| | |
| Pret | |
| | |
| | |
| 3S | 3P |
| F / C | |
| | |
| | |
| | |
| P S | |
| 1S | 1P |
| 2S | 2P |
| 3S | 3P |
| I S | |
| 1S | 1P |
| 2S | 2P |
| 3S | 3P |

Verbs exhibiting the V7 variation are affected in a fashion entirely analogous to the behavior described for variation V6, except that the vowel changes are o⇨ue and o⇨u. This could be looked at as an overlap of variation V3 (gray) with an o⇨u variation (black), except that there are no verbs that exhibit an o⇨u variation alone.

There are only two verbs families that display this V7 variation, **dormir** and **morir**. Note that the past participle of **morir, muerto,** is also irregular.

**The Verbs that exhibit the V7 variation**

| Infinitive | | | 1S-present | 3P-preterit |
|----|----|----|----|----|
| **dormir** | *to sleep* | ⇨ | **duermo** | **durmieron** |
| **entremorir** | *to die* | ⇨ | **entremuero** | **entremurieron** |
| **morir** | *to die* | ⇨ | **muero** | **murieron** |
| **morirse** | *to extinguish* | ⇨ | **me muero** | **se murieron** |

65

**Poder** exhibits both an o⇨**ue** and o⇨**u** variation, but it is categorized as one of the Truly Irregular Verbs and will be dealt with in the next chapter.

## dormir, *to sleep*

Pres.Part: **durmiendo**   Past Part: **dormido**

| Pres: | | Pret: | | Fut: |
|---|---|---|---|---|
| duermo | dormimos | dormí | dormimos | dormiré |
| duermes | dormís | dormiste | dormisteis | |
| duerme | duermen | durmió | durmieron | |
| Imp: | | | | Cond: |
| dormía | | | | dormiría |
| Pres.Sub: | | Imp.Sub: | | |
| duerma | | durmiera | durmiéramos | |
| durmamos | | durmieras | durmierais | |
| duermas | durmáis | durmiera | durmieran | |
| duerma | duerman | or | | |
| | | durmiese | durmiésemos | |
| | | durmieses | durmieseis | |
| | | durmiese | durmiesen | |

## morir, *to die*

Pres.Part: **muriendo**   Past Part: **muerto**

| Pres: | | Pret: | | Fut: |
|---|---|---|---|---|
| muero | morimos | morí | morimos | moriré |
| mueres | morís | moriste | moristeis | |
| muere | mueren | murió | murieron | |
| Imp: | | | | Cond: |
| moría | | | | moriría |
| Pres.Sub: | | Imp.Sub: | | |
| muera | muramos | muriera | muriéramos | |
| mueras | muráis | murieras | murierais | |
| muera | mueran | muriera | murieran | |
| | | or | | |
| | | muriese | muriésemos | |
| | | murieses | murieseis | |
| | | muriese | muriesen | |

# Variation Eight – V8

**Changes in base B2 (the infinitive):**
**replace the –er or –ir infinitive ending with –dr–**

**Forms affected:**
All of the future tense
All of the conditional tense

For almost all verbs, the B2 base used to form the future and conditional tenses is simply the infinitive itself, to which the endings for future and conditional tenses are added. A few verbs, however, exhibit the V8 variation in which the –er or –ir ending of the infinitive is changed to –dr– to form the B2 base.

The only verbs that exhibit the V8 variation are verbs that belong to the **valer** and **salir** families and three Truly Irregular Verbs covered in detail in chapter 4, **tener, poner** and **venir**. Note that all of these verbs also exhibit a V1 variation with the insertion of a "g" in the 1S-present and all of the present subjunctive tense. Interestingly, **asir**, the only other V1 variation verb family, does not exhibit this V8 variation.

The only other verbs that display variations in the future and conditional tenses belong to the Truly Irregular Verbs covered in the next chapter.

**The Verbs that exhibit the V8 variation**

| Infinitive | | | 1S-future |
|---|---|---|---|
| equivaler | *to equal* | ⇨ | equivaldré |
| prevaler | *to prevail* | ⇨ | prevaldré |
| resalir | *to jut out* | ⇨ | resaldré |
| salir | *to leave* | ⇨ | saldré |
| sobresalir | *to excel* | ⇨ | sobresaldré |
| valer | *to value* | ⇨ | valdré |

**salir,** *to leave*

Pres.Part: **saliendo**        Past Part: **salido**

| Pres:<br>salgo | Pret:<br>salí | Fut:<br>saldré<br>saldrás<br>saldrá | saldremos<br>saldréis<br>saldrán |
|---|---|---|---|
| Imp:<br>salía | | Cond:<br>saldría<br>saldrías<br>saldría | saldríamos<br>saldríais<br>saldrían |
| Pres.Sub:<br>salga | | Imp.Sub:<br>saliera<br>(saliese) | |

**valer,** *to value*

Pres.Part: **valiendo**        Past Part: **valido**

| Pres:<br>valgo | Pret:<br>valí | Fut:<br>valdré<br>valdrás<br>valdrá | valdremos<br>valdréis<br>valdrán |
|---|---|---|---|
| Imp:<br>valía | | Cond:<br>valdría<br>valdrías<br>valdría | valdríamos<br>valdríais<br>valdrían |
| Pres.Sub:<br>valga | | Imp.Sub:<br>valiera<br>(valiese) | |

# Variation Nine – V9

**Addition of an accent on the next to last syllable**

**Forms affected:**
 All of the present tense *except* 1P & 2P
 All of present subjunctive tense *except* 1P & 2P

Note that the forms that are affected by the V9 variation are the same as those for the V2 and V3 variations.

**Examples of V9 Verbs**

| Infinitive | | | 1S-present |
|---|---|---|---|
| **actuar** | *to act, behave* | ⇨ | **actúo** |
| **confiar** | *to trust, entrust* | ⇨ | **confío** |
| **continuar** | *to continue* | ⇨ | **continúo** |
| **contrariar** | *to oppose* | ⇨ | **contrarío** |
| **enviar** | *to send,dispatch* | ⇨ | **envío** |
| **freir** | *to fry* | ⇨ | **frío** |
| **perpetuar** | *to perpetuate* | ⇨ | **perpetúo** |
| **radiografiar** | *to take X-rays* | ⇨ | **radiografío** |
| **reir** | *to laugh* | ⇨ | **río** |
| **reunirse** | *to gather* | ⇨ | **me reúno** |
| **situar** | *to place, put* | ⇨ | **sitúo** |
| **variar** | *to vary, change* | ⇨ | **varío** |

**situar,** *to put, place*

Pres.Part.: **situando**   Past Part: **situado**

| Pres: | | Pret: | Fut: |
|---|---|---|---|
| sitúo | situamos | situé | situaré |
| sitúas | situáis | | |
| sitúa | sitúan | | |
| Imp: | | | Cond: |
| situaba | | | situaría |
| Pres.Sub: | | Imp.Sub: | |
| sitúe | situemos | situara | |
| sitúes | situéis | (situase) | |
| sitúe | sitúen | | |

### The most common verbs that exhibit the V9 variation

| | | | |
|---|---|---|---|
| actuar | *to act, behave* | extasiarse | *to become* |
| confiar | *to trust, entrust* | | *rapturous* |
| continuar | *to continue* | extenuar | *to debilitate,* |
| contrariar | *to oppose* | | *weaken* |
| criar | *to rais, breed* | extraviar | *to lead astray* |
| desconfiar | *to distrust* | fiar | *to trust, guarantee* |
| desliar | *to untie* | fluctuar | *to fluctuate,* |
| desvariar | *to be delirious* | | *hesitate* |
| desviar | *to divert, swerve* | fotografiar | *to photograph* |
| devaluar | *to devaluate* | freír | *to fry* |
| discontinuar | *to discontinue* | garuar | *to drizzle* |
| efectuar | *to bring about,* | gloriar | *to glorify* |
| | *effect* | graduar | *to graduate* |
| embaular | *to pack, cram* | guiar | *to lead, guide* |
| enfriar | *to cool, chill* | habituar | *to habituate,* |
| engreir | *to spoil, pamper* | | *accustom* |
| enhastiar | *to bore, annoy* | hastiar | *to tire, bore* |
| enriar | *to wet, soak* | infatuar (se) | *to make conceited* |
| enviar | *to send* | insinuar | *to insinuate* |
| espiar | *to spy on* | inventariar | *to take inventory* |
| esquiar | *to ski* | liar | *to tie, bind;* |
| evaluar | *to evaluate* | | *deceive* |
| exceptuar | *to exclude, exempt* | licuar | *to liquify* |
| expatriar | *to banish,* | malcriar | *to spoil, pamper* |
| | *expatriate* | mecanografiar | *to type* |

**V9 Variation Verbs (cont)**

| | | | |
|---|---|---|---|
| **menstruar** | *to menstruate* | **reunirse** | *to gather, assemble,* |
| **mimeografiar** | *to mimeograph* | | *meet* |
| **perpetuar** | *to perpetuate* | **rociar** | *to sprinkle spray* |
| **piar, piplar** | *to cheep, peep; cry,* | **sahumar** | *to perfume* |
| | *whine* | **sainar** | *to fatten* |
| **pipiar** | *to chirp* | **situar** | *to situate, place* |
| **porfiar** | *to persist, argue,* | **sofreír** | *to fry lightly* |
| | *insist* | **sonreír** | *to smile* |
| **prohijar** | *to adopt* | **taquigrafiar** | *to take shorthand* |
| **puntuar** | *to punctuate* | **tatuar** | *to tattoo* |
| **radiografiar** | *to take X-rays* | **telegrafiar** | *to telegraph* |
| **redituar** | *to produce, yield* | **triarse** | *to wear out (clothes)* |
| | *(interest)* | **usufructuar** | *to enjoy using* |
| **reenviar** | *to send back* | **vaciar** | *to empty* |
| **refreír** | *to refry* | **vaciarse** | *to spill, become* |
| **reír (se)** | *to laugh* | | *empty* |
| **repatriar** | *to repatriate* | **valuar** | *to evaluate, appraise* |
| **resfriar** | *to cool, chill* | **variar** | *to vary, shift, change* |
| **reunir** | *to join, unite* | **xerografiar** | *to Xerox®, make a* |
| | | | *copy of* |

# Variation Ten – V10
Two Special Cases: **adquirir** and **jugar**

---

**adquirir:**    **B1 and B3 base vowel change:**     i ⇨ ie

**jugar:**    **B1 and B3 base vowel change:**     u ⇨ ue

**Forms affected:**
All of the present tense *except* 1P & 2P
All of the present subjunctive tense *except* 1P & 2P

---

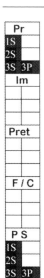

Note that the 1P and 2P forms in *both* affected tenses remain unchanged. These modifications are analogous to V2 (e⇨ie) and V3 (o⇨ue) variations and they affect the same tenses and forms as V2 and V3 as well.

There are only two common verbs that exhibit these changes.

| Infinitive | | | 1S-present |
|---|---|---|---|
| **adquirir** | *to acquire, get* | ⇨ | **adquiero** |
| **jugar** | *to play* | ⇨ | **juego** |

The full conjugation tables for both of these verbs are shown on the following page.

**adquirir,** *to acquire, obtain, get*
Pres.Part: **adquiriendo**     Past Part: **adquirido**

| Pres: | | Pret: | Fut: |
|---|---|---|---|
| adquiero | adquirimos | adquirí | adquiriré |
| adquieres | adquirís | | |
| adquiere | adquieren | | |
| Imp: | | | Cond: |
| adquiría | | | adquiriría |
| Pres.Sub: | | Imp.Sub: | |
| adquiera | adquiramos | adquiriera | |
| adquieras | adquiráis | (adquiriese) | |
| adquiera | adquieran | | |

In the table below showing the conjugation pattern for **jugar**, note the R2 (g⇨gu) spelling rule effect in the 1S-preterit and the present subjunctive tense.

**jugar,** *to play*
Pres.Part: **jugando**     Past Part: **jugado**

| Pres: | | Pret: | Fut: |
|---|---|---|---|
| juego | jugamos | jugué | jugaré |
| juegas | jugáis | | |
| juega | juegan | | |
| Imp: | | | Cond: |
| jugaba | | | jugaría |
| Pres.Sub: | | Imp.Sub: | |
| juegue | juguemos | jugara | |
| juegues | juguéis | (jugase) | |
| juegue | jueguen | | |

# Summary of the Ten Vowel Variations

---

**V1**   insert **–g–** in 1S–present and all of present subjunctive
                     **salir** ⇨ **salgo**, and **salga, salgas,...**
**V1***  insert **–ig–** in 1S–present and all of present subjunctive
                     **caer** ⇨ **caigo**, and **caiga, caigas,...**

---

**V2**   **e** ⇨ **ie**, affecting 1S, 2S, 3S, 3P–present and pres.subj.
                     **mentir** ⇨ **miento, mientes, ....**

---

**V3**   **o** ⇨ **ue**, affecting 1S, 2S, 3S, 3P–present and pres.subj.
                     **costar** ⇨ **cuesto, cuestas,...**

---

**V4**   insert **–y–** affecting 1S, 2S, 3S, 3P–present and pres.subj.,
        3S, 3P–preterit, and all of imp.subj., and pres.part.
                     **argüir** ⇨ **arguyo, arguyes,...**
                     and **arguyó** & **arguyeron**
                     and **arguyendo**

---

**V5**   **e** ⇨ **i**, affecting 1S, 2S, 3S, 3P–present, and *all* of pres.
        subj., 3S, 3P–preterit, all of imp.subj., and pres.part.
                     **colegir** ⇨ **colijo, coliges,...**
                     and **coligío** & **coligieron**
                     and **coligiendo**

---

**V6**   **e** ⇨ **ie**   affecting 1S, 2S, 3S, 3P–present and pres.subj.
        **e** ⇨ **i**    affecting 3S, 3P–preterit, 1P, 2P–present subj.,
                  all of imp.subj., and the present participle
                     **sentir** ⇨ **siento, sientes,...**
                     and **sintió** & **sintieron**
                     and **sintiendo**

---

**V7**   **o** ⇨ **ue**  affecting 1S, 2S, 3S, 3P–present and pres.subj.
        **o** ⇨ **u**   affecting 3S, 3P–preterit, 1P, 2P–present subj.,
                  all of imp.subj., and the present participle
        Only two verb families are affected: **dormir** and **morir**.
                     **dormir** ⇨ **duermo, duermes,...**
                     and **durmió** & **durmieron**
                     and **durmiendo**

---

**Summary of the 10 Variations (cont.)**

---

**V8  Replace the –er or –ir of the infinitive with a –dr– to**
        make the B2 base, affecting all of future and conditional:
Only two verb families are affected:  **salir** and **valer**
                **valer**   ⇨     **valdré**,… and **valdría**, …

---

**V9  Add accents to B1 base** in 1S, 2S, 3S, 3P–present and
                present subjunctive
                        **enviar**   ⇨   **envío, envías,**…

---

**V10  Two Special Cases:**

   **i** ⇨ **ie,** affecting 1S, 2S, 3S,3P–present and present
                subjunctive. Only 1 verb affected:
                        **adquirir** ⇨  **adquiero, adquieres,**…

   **u** ⇨ **ue,** affecting 1S, 2S, 3S, 3P–present and present
                subjunctive. Only 1 verb affected:
                        **jugar**      ⇨  **juego, juegas,**….

---

# Chapter 4

## Verb Irregularities III:
## Nineteen Truly Irregular Verbs
## and Their Families

There are only nineteen frequently encountered verb families whose conjugations depart significantly enough from the ten spelling rules and ten vowel variations to merit classification in this book as "Truly Irregular Verbs." Many of them are also affected by the spelling rules and most are members of one or more of the vowel variation types covered in chapters 2 and 3.

A **verb family** is a group of verbs that contains the same "parent" verb. For example, **tener,** *to have,* is the parent verb in a family that includes **detener,** *to delay*, **contener,** *to contain*, **mantener,** *to support*, **obtener,** *to obtain*, **sostener,** *to sustain,* and several others. Once you have learned the conjugation for **tener,** you will be able to conjugate all members of this family.

The nineteen parent verbs are listed on the following page. You should memorize this verb list so that whenever you encounter a verb belonging to these families, you will immediately recognize it as an irregular verb that has unique conjugation properties. Knowing these nineteen verbs will help you recognize nearly eighty other related verbs that belong to their families.

The most predominant characteristic of these verbs is that *there are no accents in any of the preterit forms*. No other verbs exhibit this trait. Furthermore, all but two have preterit endings that deviate in other ways from the standard pA– and pI–endings. **Dar** and **ver** both use pI–endings in their preterits, albeit without any accents (**di, diste, dio, dimos, disteis, dieron** and **vi, viste, vio, vimos, visteis, vieron**).

---

**The Nineteen Truly Irregular Verbs:**

1.  andar        *to walk*
2.  caber        *to be contained*
3.  conducir     *to lead*
4.  dar          *to give*
5.  decir        *to say*
6.  estar        *to be*
7.  haber        *to have*
8.  hacer        *to make*
9.  ir           *to go*
10. poder        *to be able*
11. poner        *to put*
12. querer       *to want*
13. saber        *to know*
14. satisfacer   *to satisfy, to know*
15. ser          *to be*
16. tener        *to hold*
17. traer        *to bring*
18. venir        *to come*
19. ver          *to see*

---

pA–endings

| 1S | 1P |
|----|----|
| 2S | 2P |
| 3S | 3P |

pI–endings

For fifteen of the remaining Truly Irregular Verbs, the preterit appears to be a mixing of the pA–endings (white cells) and pI–endings (gray cells), as shown in the diagram to the left and in the following chart.

### Preterit Endings for Most of the Truly Irregular Verbs

| 1S | –e    | 1P | –imos |
|----|-------|----|-------|
| 2S | –iste | 2P | –isteis |
| 3S | –o    | 3P | –ieron  or –eron |

The only verbs using the –**eron** 3P–preterit ending are **ser** and **ir** (both **fueron**) and **conducir, decir,** and **traer,** all three of which have preterit roots ending in "j" (giving **condujeron, dijeron,** and **trajeron**).

Strangely, **ser** and **ir** share identical preterits in all forms with unique 1S– and 3S– endings: **fui, fuiste, fue** in the singular and **fuimos, fuisteis and fueron** in the plural.

Generally speaking, the preterit base for most of these verbs has no seeming relationship to the infinitive. To work successfully with these verbs, you should memorize the 1S– and 3P–preterit forms along with the infinitive. This will give you the B4 base for the imperfect subjunctive, and also the unique base needed to make the other preterit forms.

The table below gives the list of Truly Irregular Verbs arranged so that verbs with similar preterit bases are grouped together.

### The Truly Irregular Verbs and their 3P–Preterit Forms

| | | |
|---|---|---|
| dar⇨dieron | ser⇨fueron | haber⇨hubieron |
| ver⇨vieron | ir⇨fueron | saber⇨supieron |
| | | caber⇨cupieron |
| hacer⇨hicieron | | |
| satisfacer⇨ satisficieron | querer⇨ quisieron | tener⇨tuvieron |
| | | andar⇨anduvieron |
| traer⇨trajeron | | estar⇨estuvieron |
| decir⇨dijeron | | |
| conducir⇨ condujeron | venir⇨ vinieron | poner⇨pusieron |
| | | poder⇨pudieron |

Many Truly Irregular Verbs also exhibit irregularities in the future and conditional tenses. Three (**poner, tener,** and **venir**) have the V8 variation (–**er**–ending of the infinitive becoming –**dr**–for the B2 base). Five (**querer, poder, caber, haber,** and **saber**) form their B2 bases by dropping the "e" from the infinitive, giving **querr–, podr–, cabr–, habr–** and **sabr–.** And three (**decir, hacer** and **satisfacer**) have B2 bases that are totally unique: **dir–, har–,** and **satisfar–.**

There are many similarities in the conjugations of these nineteen verbs that will make learning their conjugations easier. For one thing, the normal rules for conjugating the imperfect tense hold true for all but three verbs, **ir, ser,** and **ver.** Also, both subjunctive tenses are quite regular in their use of their respective B3 and B4 bases, keeping in mind that these bases themselves reflect irregularities in the 1S-present and 3P-preterit forms. Only four verbs, **ir, ser, haber,** and **saber,** deviate from this pattern in their present subjunctive tenses, and none deviate from the usual pattern in the imperfect subjunctive tense.

**Ir, ser,** and **haber** are the only verbs that are wildly irregular in the present tense. Others may exhibit typical V1 or V1* behavior in the present or some other 1S–present variation.

The chart below shows which of the Truly Irregular Verbs exhibit irregular properties in the various tenses not covered by the spelling rules and variations dealt with in the previous chapters.

| Pres:<br>**haber**<br>**ir**<br>**ser** | Pret:<br><br><br>**All nineteen Truly Irregular Verbs are irregular in the preterit** | Fut:<br>**decir**<br>**hacer, satisfacer**<br>**caber, saber, haber**<br>**querer, poder** |
|---|---|---|
| Imp:<br>**ir**<br>**ser**<br>**ver** | | Cond:<br>**decir**<br>**hacer, satisfacer**<br>**caber, saber, haber**<br>**querer, poder** |
| Pres.Sub:<br>**haber, ir,**<br>**saber, ser** | Imp.Sub: None, given that the 3P preterit (and therefore the B4 base) may be irregular. | |

Each of the conjugations for these verbs follows, with comments that will help in remembering their patterns. In each chart, the boxes for tenses that are conjugated regularly are shaded light gray and only the 1S form of the verb is given. The exception to this is the present tense, in which both the 1S and 2S forms are shown, since the 1S–present is most often (except for **andar**) irregular by itself.

Again, note that the two subjunctive tenses will be considered as having regular conjugation patterns if formed regularly from the B3 and B4 bases, even though these bases themselves may be irregular.

Special cases, including unusually placed accents, are highlighted in bold type. Spelling rules R1 through R9 and variations V1 through V9 are noted where appropriate.

The nineteen verbs are presented in order of increasing irregularity. The following table lists the order of presentation. **Dar, ver, andar, estar,** and **conducir** have the fewest irregularities while **haber, ser,** and **ir** have the most.

## Order of Presentation:

1. dar — *to give*
2. ver — *to see*
3. andar — *to walk*
4. estar — *to be*
5. conducir — *to lead*
6. traer — *to bring*
7. tener — *to hold*
8. venir — *to come*
9. poner — *to put*
10. querer — *to want*
11. poder — *to be able*
12. hacer — *to make*
13. satisfacer — *to satisfy, to know*
14. decir — *to say*
15. caber — *to be contained*
16. saber — *to know*
17. haber — *to have*
18. ser — *to be*
19. ir — *to go*

# dar

**Dar** is the most regular of these Truly Irregular Verbs. The B1 base for **dar** is only the single letter **d–**. **Dar** and **ver** have regular preterit conjugations, if you overlook the missing accents and the fact that **dar**, an *–ar* type verb, is using the pI–endings rather than the pA–endings. The only other deviations from regular conjugation patterns are seen in the 1S–present (**doy**) and in the accents that appear in the 1S– and 3S–present subjunctive. It's as if the accent marks simply got shifted from the preterit to the present subjunctive!

**dar,** *to give*

Pres.Part: **dando**      Past Part: **dado**

| Pres: | | | Fut: |
|---|---|---|---|
| doy | di | dimos | daré |
| das | diste | disteis | |
| Imp: | dio | dieron | Cond: |
| daba | | | daría |

| Pres.Sub: | | Imp.Sub: | |
|---|---|---|---|
| dé | demos | diera | |
| des | deis | (diese) | |
| dé | den | | |

**Note**: The 1S– and 3S–present subjunctive forms *are* accented while the 2P–present subjunctive is not.

Other common verbs belonging to this family:

**darse**      *to give one's self up*

# ver

Like **dar**, the B1 base for **ver** is only a single letter. Although "via" would work in the imperfect tense, an extra –**e**– is added, giving **veía**. Note that this same change occurs in the 1S–present form as well, which affects the B3 base and subsequently the present subjunctive.

Also like **dar**, the preterit for **ver** is perfectly regular except for the missing accents in the 1S– and 3S– forms (**vi** and **vio**, respectively). However, the past participle is completely unique.

**ver,** *to see*

Pres.Part: **viendo**    Past Part: **visto**

| Pres: | | Pret: | | Fut: |
|---|---|---|---|---|
| veo | | vi | vimos | veré |
| ves | | viste | visteis | |
| Imp: | | vio | vieron | Cond: |
| veía | veíamos | | | vería |
| veías | veíais | | | |
| veía | veían | | | |
| Pres.Sub: | | Imp.Sub: | | |
| vea | | viera | | |
| | | (viese) | | |

Other common verbs belonging to this family include

| **entrever** | to glimpse, surmise |
|---|---|
| **prever** | to foresee |
| **rever** | to review, revise |

# andar and estar

The conjugations for **andar** and **estar** are also quite simple. In fact, for **andar** the only irregularity is the preterit tense, while for **estar**, the 1S–present (**estoy**), the preterit and the V9 accent variations mark the only irregularities.

**andar,** *to walk*

Pres.Part: **andando**     Past Part: **andado**

| Pres: | Pret: | | Fut: |
|---|---|---|---|
| **ando** | **anduve** | **anduvimos** | **andaré** |
| **andas** | **anduviste** | **anduvisteis** | |
| Imp: | **anduvo** | **anduvieron** | Cond: |
| **andaba** | | | **andaría** |
| Pres.Sub: | | Imp.Sub: | |
| **ande** | | **anduviera** | |
| | | **(anduviese)** | |

Other common verbs belonging to this family include

**desandar**     *to retrace one's steps*

**estar,** *to be*  **V9**

Pres.Part: **estando**     Past Part: **estado**

| Pres: | Pret: | | Fut: |
|---|---|---|---|
| **estoy** | **estuve** | **estuvimos** | **estaré** |
| **estás** | **estuviste** | **estuvisteis** | |
| Imp: | **estuvo** | **estuvieron** | Cond: |
| **estaba** | | | **estaría** |
| Pres.Sub: | | Imp.Sub: | |
| **esté** | | **estuviera** | |
| | | **(estuviese)** | |

Other common verbs belonging to this family: none.

# conducir

**Conducir** is also quite regular except for the preterit, taking into account the R5 spelling rule component (**c⇨zc**) in its 1S–present and present subjunctive spellings. Note the missing –**i**– in the 3P–preterit.

**conducir,** *to conduct, lead* - **R5**
Pres.Part: **conduciendo**   Past Part: **conducido**

| Pres: | Pret: | | Fut: |
|---|---|---|---|
| **conduzco** | **conduje** | **condujimos** | **conduciré** |
| **conduces** | **condujiste** | **condujisteis** | |
| Imp: | **condujo** | **condujeron** | Cond: |
| **conducía** | | | **conduciría** |
| Pres.Sub: | | Imp.Sub: | |
| **conduzca** | | **condujera** | |
| | | **(condujese)** | |

Other common verbs belonging to this family include

| | |
|---|---|
| **abducir** | *to abduct* |
| **deducir** | *to deduce* |
| **inducir** | *to persuade* |
| **introducir** | *to introduce* |
| **producir** | *to produce* |
| **reducir** | *to reduce* |
| **reproducir** | *to reproduce* |
| **seducir** | *to seduce* |
| **traducir** | *to translate* |

# traer

**Traer** exhibits a V1* modification to its 1S–present that is reflected throughout the present subjunctive of this verb. The present participle exhibits an R9 modification, replacing the –i–with a –**y**–.

**traer,** *to bring*   **R9, V1***

Pres.Part: **trayendo**         Past Part: **traído**

| Pres: | Pret: | | Fut: |
|---|---|---|---|
| traigo | traje | trajimos | traeré |
| traes | trajiste | trajisteis | |
| | trajo | trajeron | |
| Imp: | | | Cond: |
| traía | | | traería |
| Pres.Sub: | | Imp.Sub: | |
| traiga | | trajera | |
| | | (trajese) | |

Other common verbs belonging to this family include

| abstraer | *to abstract* |
|---|---|
| atraer | *to attract* |
| contraer | *to contract* |
| detraer | *to defame* |
| distraer | *to distract* |
| extraer | *to extract* |
| maltraer | *to abuse* |
| retraer | *to retract* |
| retrotraer | *to antedate* |
| substraer | *to subtract* |
| sustraer | *to subtract* |

# tener

**Tener** is often considered to be one of the most irregular verbs in Spanish. Like **andar** and **estar**, it does have a "uv" in its preterit base. But all of the other irregularities fit tidily in the context of vowel variations discussed in the previous chapter. **Tener** exhibits a V1 varient (insert –g– in the 1S–present) which then affects the present subjunctive, and it has a V2 (e⇨ie) component. It also exhibits a V8 component (–dr– substitution in the infinitive) to form the B2 base. Since the V1 variation trumps all others in the present subjunctive, **tener** does not have the e⇨ie change in that tense. Thus only three forms, the 2S, 3S, and 3P–present, exhibit the e⇨ie change.

      **Tener** and **venir** both share V1, V2, and V8 characteristics.

**tener,** *to have, to hold* – **V1, V2, V8**

Pres.Part: **teniendo**     Past Part: **tenido**

| Pres: <br> tengo <br> tienes | Pret: <br> tuve    tuvimos <br> tuviste    tuvisteis <br> tuvo    tuvieron | Fut: <br> tendré |
|---|---|---|
| Imp: <br> tenía | | Cond: <br> tendría |
| Pres.Sub: <br> tenga | Imp.Sub: <br> tuviera <br> (tuviese) | |

Other common verbs belonging to this family include

| | |
|---|---|
| **abstenerse** | *to abstain* |
| **atenerse** | *to rely on* |
| **contener** | *to contain* |
| **detener** | *to stop* |
| **entretener** | *to entertain, to amuse* |
| **mantener** | *to support* |
| **obtener** | *to obtain, to get* |
| **retener** | *to retain* |
| **sostener** | *to sustain* |

# venir

Like **tener, venir** exhibits V1, V2 and V8 variations. With the exception of the preterit, most of **venir**'s irregularities are categorized under the common vowel variations described in the previous chapter. Thus the V1 variation affecting the 1S–present is reflected in the present subjunctive, trumping the V2 variation, which thus only affects the 2S, 2P, and 3P–present forms.

Do not confuse the **e**⇨**i** change in **venir** with the typical V5 or V6 variations. For **venir**, this change affects the entire preterit (not just the 3S and 3P forms), the imperfect subjunctive (of course), and the present participle. It does not show up in the present subjunctive at all.

**venir,** *to come –* **V1, V2, V8**

Pres.Part: **viniendo**     Past Part: **venido**

| Pres: vengo vienes | Pret: vine   vinimos viniste vinisteis vino   vinieron | Fut: vendré |
|---|---|---|
| Imp: venía | | Cond: vendría |
| Pres.Sub: venga | Imp.Sub: viniera (viniese) | |

Other common verbs belonging to this family include

| advenir | *to arrive* |
|---|---|
| avenir | *to reconcile* |
| convenir | *to agree* |
| devenir | *to happen, come about* |
| disconvenir | *to disagree, differ in opinion* |
| intervenir | *to intervene* |
| prevenir | *to prevent* |
| provenir | *to originate* |
| revenir | *to return* |
| sobrevenir | *to occur later* |
| subvenir | *to provide for needs* |
| supervenir | *to happen* |

# poner

**Poner** has the largest of the verb families associated with the Truly Irregular Verbs. All of the verbs in this family share identical V1 characteristics (insertion of –**g**– in the 1S–present) as well as the irregular preterit and unusual past participle, the only form to exhibit an **o**⇨**ue** change.

**poner,** *to put, to place* – **V1, V8**

Pres.Part: **poniendo**          Past Part: **puesto**

| Pres: | | Pret: | | Fut: |
|---|---|---|---|---|
| pongo | | puse | pusimos | pondré |
| pones | | pusiste | pusisteis | |
| | | puso | pusieron | |
| Imp: | | | | Cond: |
| ponía | | | | pondría |
| Pres.Sub: | | | Imp.Sub: | |
| ponga | | | pusiera | |
| | | | (pusiese) | |

Other common verbs belonging to this family include

| | | | |
|---|---|---|---|
| **anteponer** | *to prefer* | **ponerse** | *to dress* |
| **componer** | *to compose* | **posponer** | *to postpone* |
| **contraponer** | *to compare, to oppose* | **predisponer** | *to bias* |
| | | **presuponer** | *to presuppose, to budget* |
| **deponer** | *to lay aside, to depose* | **proponer** | *to propose* |
| **descomponer** | *to disarrange, disrupt, disturb* | **recomponer** | *to fix, repair* |
| | | **reponer** | *to put back* |
| **disponer** | *to dispose* | **sobreponer** | *to superimpose* |
| **exponer** | *to expose* | **superponer** | *to superimpose* |
| **imponer** | *to impose* | **suponer** | *to assume* |
| **indisponer** | *to make ill* | **transponer** | *to transfer, to transpose* |
| **interponer** | *to interpose* | | |
| **oponer** | *to oppose* | **yuxtaponer** | *to juxtapose* |

# querer

**Querer** exhibits the **e⇨ie** vowel modification in the present and present subjunctive tenses typical of a V2 verb.

The B2 base that governs the future and conditional for **querer** is formed by dropping the "e" in the infinitive ending. This change is only observed among some of the Truly Irregular Verbs (**poder, caber, saber,** and **haber)** and their verb families. It is not found elsewhere.

Note that the only distinction between the imperfect and conditional forms for **querer** is a single or a double "r." This unusual similarity is due to dropping the "e" from the infinitive to form the B2 base.

**querer,** *to want, to wish –* **V2**

Pres.Part: **queriendo**         Past Part: **querido**

| Pres:<br>quiero<br>quieres | Pret:<br>quise<br>quisiste | quisimos<br>quisisteis | Fut:<br>querré |
|---|---|---|---|
| Imp:<br>quería | quiso | quisieron | Cond:<br>querría |
| Pres.Sub:<br>quiera | | Imp.Sub:<br>quisiera<br>(quisiese) | |

Other common verbs belonging to this family include

**malquerer**     to dislike

# poder

**Poder** drops an "e" from the infinitive to form the B2 base that governs the future and conditional tenses. This change is also observed in other Truly Irregular Verbs (**querer, caber, saber, haber**) and their verb families, but is not found elsewhere.

**Poder** could be considered similar to the two V7 verbs, **dormir** and **morir**, which also exhibit the combination of **o⇨ue** and **o⇨u** vowel changes. The difference is that **poder** incorporates the **o⇨u** modification throughout the preterit, while the V7 verbs show that change only in the 3S and 3P–preterit forms.

The present participle also reflects the **o⇨u** modification. A similar vowel carryover from the preterit to the present participle is observed by **venir** as well.

**poder,** *to be able, can* – **V3**

Pres.Part: **pudiendo**       Past Part: **podido**

| Pres: puedo puedes | Pret: pude pudimos pudiste pudisteis pudo pudieron | Fut: podré |
|---|---|---|
| Imp: podía | | Cond: podría |
| Pres.Sub: pueda | Imp.Sub: pudiera (pudiese) | |

Other common verbs belonging to this family: none.

# hacer

The first thing you encounter with **hacer** is the strange 1S–present form. At first may you think that this is an example of variation V1 with insertion of a –**g**– in the 1S–present. Closer inspection reveals that the "g" has replaced a "c." As usual, the 1S–present dictates the structure of the B3 base, so this change is reflected throughout the present subjunctive.

**Hacer** has an unusual B2 base formed by dropping the "ce" from the infinitive, creating **har**–. This leads to irregularities throughout the future and conditional tenses.

The 3S–preterit form, **hizo**, is the only place in **hacer**'s conjugation where the R5* (**c**⇨**z**) spelling rule appears.

**Hacer** also displays an uncommon variation in its past participle; **hecho**.

**hacer,** *to make, to do* – **R5***

Pres.Part: **haciendo**    Past Part: **hecho**

| Pres: | Pret: | | Fut: | |
|---|---|---|---|---|
| hago | hice | hicimos | haré | haremos |
| haces | hiciste | hicisteis | harás | haréis |
| | hizo | hicieron | hará | harán |
| Imp: | | | Cond: | |
| hacía | | | haría | haríamos |
| | | | harías | haríais |
| | | | haría | harían |
| Pres.Sub: | | | Imp.Sub: | |
| haga | | | hiciera | |
| | | | (hiciese) | |

Other common verbs belonging to this family include

| | |
|---|---|
| **contrahacer** | *to imitate* |
| **deshacer** | *to undo, to destroy* |
| **rehacer** | *to redo, to remake* |

# satisfacer

**Satisfacer** is conjugated following the pattern exhibited by **hacer**. It shows the same replacement of a "c" with a "g" in the 1S–present form that is seen with **hacer**. Like **hacer, satisfacer** has an unusual B2 base formed by dropping the "ce" from the infinitive, creating **satisfar–**. This leads to irregularities throughout the future and conditional tenses.

Both verbs also share the preterit base ending in "ic," the R5* c⇨z change in the 3S–preterit, and the **–cho** ending in their past participles.

**satisfacer,** *to satisfy – R5\**

Pres.Part: **satisfaciendo**   Past Part: **satisfecho**

| Pres:<br>satisfago,<br>satisfaces | Pret:<br>satisfice satisficimos<br>satisficiste satisficisteis<br>satisfizo satisficieron |
| --- | --- |
| | Fut:<br>satisfaré satisfaremos<br>satisfarás satisfaréis<br>satisfará satisfarán |
| Imp:<br>satisfacía | Cond:<br>satisfaría satisfaríamos<br>satisfarías satisfaríais<br>satisfaría satisfarían |
| Pres.Sub:<br>satisfaga | Imp.Sub:<br>satisficiera<br>(satisficiese) |

Other common verbs belonging to this family: none.

# decir

**Decir** exhibits a V5 (e⇨i) variation, and forms its 1S–present by substituting a "g" for the "c," giving **digo**. This change is then reflected throughout the present subjunctive.

For the B2 base, **decir** drops the "ci" from the infinitive, and changes the remaining vowel to an "i," giving **dir–**. In fact, the future and conditional are formed as though the verb infinitive should have been "dir."

Note that the e⇨i change is observed in all forms in all tenses except the imperfect and the 1P and 2P-present, which are **decimos** and **decís**.

Like **hacer** and **satisfacer, decir**  and **redecir** share the uncommon variation in their past participles, which end in –**cho**. The other **decir** family verbs all have regular past participles. For example, **bendecir** ⇨ bendecido.

**decir,** *to say, to tell* – **V5**

Pres.Part: **diciendo**        Past Part: **dicho**

| Pres: | Pret: | | Fut: | |
|---|---|---|---|---|
| **digo** | **dije** | **dijimos** | **diré** | **diremos** |
| **dices** | **dijiste** | **dijisteis** | **dirás** | **diréis** |
| | **dijo** | **dijeron** | **dirá** | **dirán** |
| Imp: | | | Cond: | |
| **decía** | | | **diría** | **diríamos** |
| | | | **dirías** | **diríais** |
| | | | **diría** | **dirían** |
| Pres.Sub: | | Imp.Sub: | | |
| **diga** | | **dijera** | | |
| | | **(dijese)** | | |

Other common verbs belonging to this family include

| **bendecir** | *to bless* |
|---|---|
| **contradecir** | *to contradict* |
| **entredecir** | *to prohibit, interdict* |
| **interdecir** | *to interdict, prohibit* |
| **maldecir** | *to curse* |
| **predecir** | *to predict* |
| **redecir** | *to repeat, say again* |

# caber

One would think that **caber, saber,** and **haber** would be very similar in conjugation across all tenses. All three do exhibit the same irregularity in the formation of the B2 base (the "e" is dropped from the infinitive, just like **poder** and **querer**). Beyond this similarity, they are all quite different. **Caber** has an unusual 1S–present (affecting the present subjunctive) and is, of course, irregular in its preterit. At least both of its participles are regular!

**caber,** *to be contained, to fit into*

Pres.Part: **cabiendo**    Past Part: **cabido**

| Pres: | Pret: | | Fut: |
|---|---|---|---|
| quepo | cupe | cupimos | cabré |
| cabes | cupiste | cupisteis | |
| **Imp:** | cupo | cupieron | **Cond:** |
| cabía | | | cabría |
| **Pres.Sub:** | | **Imp.Sub:** | |
| quepa | | cupiera | |
| | | (cupiese) | |

Common verbs belonging to this family: none.

# saber

The 1S–present for **saber** is quite irregular and has an accent over the "e" that does *not* carry over into the present subjunctive, since the present subjunctive tense does *not* use the regular B3 base, but constructs one of its very own, **sep-**.

Like **caber, haber, poder,** and **querer,** the B2 base that governs the future and conditional for **saber** is formed by dropping the "e" in the infinitive ending, giving **sabr–**.

**saber,** *to know, to know how*

Pres.Part: **sabiendo**      Past Part: **sabido**

| Pres: | Pret: | | Fut: | |
|---|---|---|---|---|
| sé | supe | supimos | sabré | sabremos |
| sabes | supiste | supisteis | sabrás | sabréis |
| | supo | supieron | sabrá | sabrán |
| Imp: | | | Cond: | |
| sabía | | | sabría | sabríamos |
| | | | sabrías | sabríais |
| | | | sabría | sabrían |
| Pres.Sub: | | | Imp.Sub: | |
| sepa | sepamos | | supiera | |
| sepas | sepáis | | (supiese) | |
| sepa | sepan | | | |

Common verbs belonging to this family include

**resaber**    *to know well*

# haber

The B2 base that governs the future and conditional for **haber** is formed by dropping the "e" in the infinitive ending, similar to **caber, saber, poder,** and **querer.**

Like **saber,** the 1S–present has no relation to the forms in the present subjunctive. However, both participles are formed normally.

**Haber,** in its various tenses, is used with the past participle of other verbs to form the seven compound tenses (Chapter 5). All seven of **haber**'s simple tenses are used in these constructions. For example:

| | |
|---|---|
| **Hemos comido.** | *We have eaten.* |
| **Él ya había comido.** | *He had already eaten.* |
| **Habrán comido.** | *They will have eaten.* |

Thus **haber** is one of the most used verbs in Spanish, and it is essential that its full conjugation pattern be thoroughly memorized.

**haber,** *has, have, had*

Pres.Part: **habiendo**      Past Part: **habido**

| Pres: | | Pret: | | Fut: | |
|---|---|---|---|---|---|
| he | hemos | hube | hubimos | habré | habremos |
| has | habéis | hubiste | hubisteis | habrás | habréis |
| ha | han | hubo | hubieron | habrá | habrán |

| Imp: | | | | Cond: | |
|---|---|---|---|---|---|
| había | | | | habría | habríamos |
| | | | | habrías | habríais |
| | | | | habría | habrían |

| Pres.Sub: | | Imp.Sub: | |
|---|---|---|---|
| haya | hayamos | hubiera | |
| hayas | hayáis | (hubiese) | |
| haya | hayan | | |

Common verbs belonging to this family: none.

# ser

The future, conditional and imperfect subjunctive tenses and the participles are conjugated regularly for **ser**. All of the other tenses are irregular, even the imperfect. The preterit endings do not follow the usual preterit pattern for the Truly Irregular Verbs. Note that the 2S and 3S–present forms for **ser** have a different base than the other present forms. Also note the very strange feature that the preterit (and hence the imperfect subjunctive) tenses for both **ser** and **ir** are identical!

**Note:** The 1P–imperfect has an accent over the "e."

**ser,** *to be*

Pres.Part: **siendo**      Past Part: **sido**

| Pres: | | Pret: | | Fut: |
|---|---|---|---|---|
| soy | somos | fui | fuimos | seré |
| eres | sois | fuiste | fuisteis | |
| es | son | fue | fueron | |
| Imp: | | | | Cond: |
| era | éramos | | | sería |
| eras | erais | | | |
| era | eran | | | |
| Pres.Sub: | | Imp.Sub: | | |
| sea | seamos | fuera | | |
| seas | seáis | (fuese) | | |
| sea | sean | | | |

Common verbs belonging to this family: none.

# ir

Like **ser**, the future, conditional and imperfect subjunctive tenses are conjugated regularly for **ir**. All other tenses are irregular. Both **ir** and **ser** have the same preterit and imperfect subjunctive forms. Distinguishing between them in actual use is strictly a matter of context.

Like **haber**, **ir** is also used as an auxiliary verb in compound constructions that would be translated "going to…," as in "They are going to speak." (See Chapter 6.) The appropriate present or imperfect form of **ir** is used along with the preposition **a** and the infinitive of the action verb to create this mood. For example:

| | |
|---|---|
| **Van a hablar.** | *They are going to speak.* |
| **Ella iba a leer el libro ayer.** | *She was going to read the book yesterday.* |

**Note:** The 1P–imperfect has an accent over the "i."

**ir,** *to go*

Pres.Part: **yendo**      Past Part: **ido**

| Pres: | | Pret: | | Fut: |
|---|---|---|---|---|
| voy | vamos | fui | fuimos | iré |
| vas | vais | fuiste | fuisteis | |
| va | van | fue | fueron | |

| Imp: | | | | Cond: |
|---|---|---|---|---|
| iba | íbamos | | | iría |
| ibas | ibais | | | |
| iba | iban | | | |

| Pres.Sub: | | Imp.Sub: |
|---|---|---|
| vaya | vayamos | fuera |
| vayas | vayáis | (fuese) |
| vaya | vayan | |

Other common verbs belonging to this family: none

# Summary of Conjugation Irregularities for the Truly Irregular Verbs

| Except as noted below, the preterit endings for the Truly Irregular Verbs are: | 1S | –e | 1P | –imos |
|---|---|---|---|---|
| | 2S | –iste | 2P | –isteis |
| | 3S | –o | 3P | –ieron or –eron |

**Note**: The present subjunctive and imperfect subjunctive tenses are taken to be regularly conjugated if they follow standard conjugation patterns even though their respective bases may be irregular.

| | |
|---|---|
| 1.**dar**<br>*to give* | » 1S–present: **doy**<br>» 1S and 3S–present subjunctive are accented:  **dé**<br>» preterit conjugated as a normal *–er/–ir* verb,<br>but with no accents: <u>**di**</u>, **diste**, <u>**dio**</u>…**dieron** |
| 2.**ver**<br>*to see* | » 1S–present has an added "e: **v<u>e</u>o**<br>» imperfect displays an added "e" in all forms:<br>**v<u>e</u>ía, v<u>e</u>ías**…<br>» preterit conjugated as a normal *–er/–ir* verb,<br>but with no accents: <u>**vi**</u>, **viste**, <u>**vio**</u>…**vieron**<br>» past participle: **visto** |
| 3.**andar**<br>*to walk* | » preterit base is **anduv–**: **anduve… anduvieron** |
| 4.**estar**<br>*to be* | » 1S–present:   **estoy**<br>» present and present subjunctive exhibit V9<br>accents: **estás…** and   **esté…**<br>» preterit base is **estuv–**: **estuve… estuvieron** |
| 5.**conducir**<br>*to conduct* | »1S–present: **conduzco** (R5)<br>» preterit base is **conduj–**:<br>**conduje…<u>condujeron</u>** |
| 6.**traer**<br>*to bring* | » 1S–present: **traigo** (V1*)<br>» preterit base is **traj–**: **traje…** <u>**trajeron**</u><br>» present participle is **trayendo** (R9) |

7. **tener**
*to hold*
» 1S–present: **tengo** (V1)
» present exhibits a V2 modification (**e**⇨**ie**)
   in 2S, 3S, and 3P: **tienes, tiene** and **tienen**
» future and conditional have a V8 modification:
   **tendré...** and **tendría...**
» preterit base is **tuv–**: **tuve...tuvieron**

8. **venir**
*to come*
» 1S–present: **vengo** (V1)
» present exhibits a V2 modification (**e**⇨**ie**)
   in 2S, 3S, and 3P: **vienes, viene and vienen**
» future and conditional have a V8 modification:
   **vendré...** and **vendría...**
» preterit base is **vin–**: **vine...vinieron**
» present participle: **viniendo**

9. **poner**
*to put*
» 1S–present: **pongo** (V1)
» future and conditional have a V8 modification:
   **pondré...** and **pondría...**
» preterit base is **pus–**: **puse...pusieron**
» past participle: **puesto**

10. **querer**
*to want*
» present and present subjunctive exhibit a V2
   modification (**e**⇨**ie**) in the 1S, 2S, 3S, and 3P:
   **quiero...** and **quiera...**
» future and conditional have an irregular base in
   which the "e" from the infinitive is dropped:
   **querré...** and **querría...**
» preterit base is **quis–**: **quise...quisieron**

11. **poder**
*to be able*
» present and present subjunctive exhibit a V3
   modification (**o**⇨**ue**) in the 1S, 2S, 3S, and 3P:
   **puedo...** and **pueda...**
» future and conditional have an irregular base
   in which the "e" from the infinitive is dropped:
   **podré...** and **podría...**
» preterit base is **pud–**: **pude...pudieron**
» present participle: **pudiendo**

12. **hacer** » 1S–present: **hago**
*to make* » future and conditional have an irregular
base, **har–**, leading to: **haré...** and **haría...**
» preterit base is **hic–**: **hice...hicieron**
with an R5 component in the 3S: **hizo**
» past participle: **hecho**

13. **satisfacer** » 1S–present: **satisfago**
*to satisfy* » future and conditional have an irregular
base, **satisfar–**, leading to:
**satisfaré...** and **satisfaría...**
» preterit base is **satisfic–**:
**satisfice...satisficieron**
with an R5 component in the 3S: **satisfizo**
» past participle: **satisfecho**

14. **decir** » 1S–present: **digo**
*to say* » future and conditional have **dir–** for a base
leading to: **diré...** and **diría...**
» preterit base is **dij–**: **dije...dijeron**
» past participle: **dicho**

15. **caber** » 1S–present: **quepo**
*to be* » future and conditional have an irregular base
*contained* in which the "e" from the infinitive is dropped:
**cabré...** and **cabría...**
» preterit base is **cup–**: **cupe...cupieron**

16. **saber** » 1S–present: **sé**
*to know* » future and conditional have an irregular base in which
the "e" from the infinitive is dropped:
**sabré...** and **sabría...**
» present subjunctive base is **sep–**: **sepa...sepan**
» preterit base is **sup–**: **supe...supieron**

17. **haber** » present: **he, has, ha & hemos, habéis, han.**
*to have* » future and conditional have an irregular base
in which the "e" from the infinitive is dropped:
**habré...** and **habría...**
» present subjunctive base is **hay–**: **haya...hayan**
» preterit base is **hub–**: **hube...hubieron**

18. **ser** » present: **soy, eres, es & somos, sois, son**
   *to be* » imperfect:

   **era, eras, era & éramos, erais, eran**
   » present subjunctive base is **se–: sea...sean**
   » preterit has a totally unique conjugation that is
   shared with **ir** and is displayed in the table below:

19. **ir** » present: **voy, vas, va & vamos, vais, van**
   *to be* » imperfect:

   **iba, ibas, iba & íbamos, ibais, iban**
   » present subjunctive base is **vay–: vaya...vayan**
   » preterit has a totally unique conjugation that is
   shared with **ser** and is displayed in the table below:

### The preterit conjugation for ser and ir

| 1S | fui | 1P | fuimos |
|----|--------|----|----------|
| 2S | fuiste | 2P | fuisteis |
| 3S | fue | 3P | fueron |

# Chapter 5

## Irregular Participles

Participles are among the most widely used verb forms in Spanish. Fortunately, most have regular constructions corresponding to the rules outlined in chapter one. These rules are shown again here:

> **Present Participle Formation:**
>
> **Base B1 + ending (no link).**
>     *–ar* **verbs end in** –ando;
>     *–er/–ir* **verbs end in** –iendo.

> **Past Participle Formation:**
>
> **Base B1 + ending (no link).**
>     *–ar* **verbs end in** –ado;
>     *–er/–ir* **verbs end in** –ido.

Where spelling rules are called into play, particularly R8 and R9, participles conform without exception. Similarly, variations V4, V5, and V6 involve vowel changes that are reflected in the present participles. To review:

**R8**: The –i– in the present participle's ending is dropped if it follows an –ll– or –ñ–. Thus:

| | | | | | |
|---|---|---|---|---|---|
| **bullir** | *to boil* | ⇨ | **bullendo** | and | **bullido** |
| **uñir** | *to yoke* | ⇨ | **uñendo** | and | **uñido** |

**R9**: The –i– in the present participle's ending is replaced with a –y– if it follows an –a–, –e–, or –o– or it is dropped if it would result in a double "i." Thus:

| | | | | | |
|---|---|---|---|---|---|
| **caer** | *to fall* | ⇨ | **cayendo** | and | **caído** |
| **reír** | *to laugh* | ⇨ | **riendo** | and | **reído** |
| **traer** | *to try* | ⇨ | **trayendo** | and | **traído** |

**V4**: A –y– replaces the –i– in the present participle's ending. The past participle is formed regularly. Thus:

| | | | | | |
|---|---|---|---|---|---|
| **oir** | *to see* | ⇨ | **oyendo** | and | **oído** |
| **fluir** | *to flow* | ⇨ | **fluyendo** | and | **fluído** |

**V5, V6 and V7**: The present participles for these verbs have the **e**⇨**i** or **o**⇨**u** change in the base forming their present participles. The past participles retain the "e" or "o" spellings Some Truly Irregular Verbs fall into this category, too. Thus:

| | | | | | |
|---|---|---|---|---|---|
| **mentir** | *to lie* | ⇨ | **mintiendo** | and | **mentido** |
| **medir** | *to measure* | ⇨ | **midiendo** | and | **medido** |
| **venir** | *to come* | ⇨ | **viniendo** | and | **venido** |
| **dormir** | *to sleep* | ⇨ | **durmiendo** | and | **dormido** |
| **poder** | *to be able* | ⇨ | **pudiendo** | and | **podido** |

There are a few verbs that have irregular participles that do not fall into any of the above categories. For these, the basic structures follow no common pattern. Your only recourse is simply to study them until they become familiar to you. However, there are only fourteen verb families that fall in this category, and you have encountered six of them already as Truly Irregular Verbs.

These verbs are listed below with both their present and past participles. Most show irregularities in only one participle, so those that are regular are shown in gray while the irregular participles are highlighted in bold. The verbs are listed according to verb families in order to emphasize the relationship between the verbs and to simplify the familiarization process.

| Infinitive | | Present Participle | Past Participle |
|---|---|---|---|
| **abrir** | | | |
| **abrir,** *to open* | ⇨ | abriendo | **abierto** |
| **entreabrir,** *to set ajar* | ⇨ | entreabriendo | **entreabierto** |
| **cubrir** | | | |
| **cubrir,** *to cover* | ⇨ | cubriendo | **cubierto** |
| **descubrir,** *to discover* | ⇨ | descubriendo | **descubierto** |
| **encubrir,** *to conceal* | ⇨ | encubriendo | **encubierto** |
| **decir** | | | |
| **decir,** *to say* | ⇨ | **diciendo** | **dicho** |
| **redecir,** *to say again* | ⇨ | **rediciendo** | **redicho** |
| **hacer** | | | |
| **contrahacer,** *to imitate* | ⇨ | contrahaciendo | **contrahecho** |
| **deshacer,** *to undo* | ⇨ | deshaciendo | **deshecho** |
| **hacer,** *to make, do* | ⇨ | haciendo | **hecho** |
| **rehacer,** *to do over* | ⇨ | rehaciendo | **rehecho** |
| **ir,** *to go* | ⇨ | **yendo** | **ido** |
| **morir** | | | |
| **entremorir,** *to die out* | ⇨ | **entremuriendo** | **entremuerto** |
| **morir,** *to die out* | ⇨ | **muriendo** | **muerto** |
| **poner** | | | |
| **anteponer,** *to prefer* | ⇨ | anteponiendo | **antepuesto** |
| **componer,** *to compose* | ⇨ | componiendo | **compuesto** |
| **contraponer,** *to compare* | ⇨ | contraponiendo | **contrapuesto** |
| **deponer,** *to lay aside* | ⇨ | deponiendo | **depuesto** |
| **descomponer,** *to disrupt* | ⇨ | descomponiendo | **descompuesto** |
| **disponer,** *to dispose* | ⇨ | disponiendo | **dispuesto** |
| **exponer,** *to expose* | ⇨ | exponiendo | **expuesto** |
| **imponer,** *to impose* | ⇨ | imponiendo | **impuesto** |

| Infinitive | | Present Participle | Past Participle |
|---|---|---|---|
| **poner** (cont.) | | | |
| **indisponer,** *to make ill* | ⇨ | indisponiendo | **indispuesto** |
| **interponer,** *to interpose* | ⇨ | interponiendo | **interpuesto** |
| **oponer,** *to oppose* | ⇨ | oponiendo | **opuesto** |
| **poner,** *to put, place* | ⇨ | poniendo | **puesto** |
| **ponerse,** *to dress* | ⇨ | poniéndose | **puesto** |
| **posponer,** *to postpone* | ⇨ | posponiendo | **pospuesto** |
| **predisponer,** *to bias* | ⇨ | predisponiendo | **predispuesto** |
| **presuponer,** *to presuppose, to budget* | ⇨ | presuponiendo | **presupuesto** |
| **proponer,** *to propose* | ⇨ | proponiendo | **propuesto** |
| **recomponer,** *repair* | ⇨ | recomponiendo | **recompuesto** |
| **reponer,** *to put back* | ⇨ | reponiendo | **repuesto** |
| **sobreponer,** *to superimpose* | ⇨ | sobreponiendo | **sobrepuesto** |
| **superponer,** *to superimpose* | ⇨ | superponiendo | **superpuesto** |
| **suponer,** *to assume* | ⇨ | suponiendo | **supuesto** |
| **transponer,** *to transfer* | ⇨ | transponiendo | **transpuesto** |
| **yuxtaponer,** *to juxtapose* | ⇨ | yuxtaponiendo | **yuxtapuesto** |
| **(primir)** | | | |
| **imprimir,** *to print* | ⇨ | imprimiendo | **impreso** |
| **reimprimir,** *to reprint* | ⇨ | reimprimiendo | **reimpreso** |
| **romper,** *to break* | ⇨ | rompiendo | **roto** |
| **satisfacer,** *to satisfy* | ⇨ | satisfaciendo | **satisfecho** |

| Infinitive | | Present Participle | Past Participle |
|---|---|---|---|
| **(scribir)** | | | |
| **adscribir,** *to assign* | ⇨ | adscribiendo | **adscrito** |
| **describir,** *to describe* | ⇨ | describiendo | **descrito** |
| **escribir,** *to write* | ⇨ | escribiendo | **escrito** |
| **inscribir,** *to register* | ⇨ | inscribiendo | **inscrito** |
| **proscribir,** *to banish* | ⇨ | proscribiendo | **proscrito** |
| **subscribir,** *to subscribe* | ⇨ | subscribiendo | **subscrito** |
| **transcribir,** *to transcribe* | ⇨ | transcribiendo | **transcrito** |
| **(solver)** | | | |
| **absolver,** *to absolve* | ⇨ | absolviendo | **absuelto** |
| **disolver,** *to dissolve* | ⇨ | disolviendo | **disuelto** |
| **resolver,** *to solve* | ⇨ | resolviendo | **resuelto** |
| **ver** | | | |
| **entrever,** *to glimpse* | ⇨ | entreviendo | **entrevisto** |
| **prever,** *to foresee* | ⇨ | previendo | **previsto** |
| **rever,** *to review, revise* | ⇨ | reviendo | **revisto** |
| **ver,** *to see* | ⇨ | viendo | **visto** |
| **volver** | | | |
| **revolver,** *to mix, stir* | ⇨ | revolviendo | **revuelto** |
| **volver,** *to turn* | ⇨ | volviendo | **vuelto** |

# Chapter 6

## Regular Verb Conjugation II:
## The Seven Compound Tenses

The seven compound tenses are those that require the use of some form of the auxiliary verb **haber,** *to have,* combined with the past participle of the action verb. They are translated into English with "have," "has," "had," "will have," or "would have." Each compound tense corresponds to one of the seven simple tenses.

Thus the present perfect tense ("have") uses the present tense forms of **haber** plus the past participle of the desired verb; the pluperfect ("had") tense uses the imperfect tense forms of **haber** plus the past participle; the future perfect ("will have") tense uses the future tense forms of **haber** plus the past participle.

In order to construct the compound tenses, you must know thoroughly the full conjugation of **haber** in its seven simple tenses. Of course, you must know how to form the past participles for the verbs you wish to use with **haber,** as described in chapter one:

---

**Past Participle Formation:**

**Base B1 + ending (no link).**
  *–ar* **verbs end in  –ado;**
  *–er–/ir* **verbs end in   –ido.**

---

Since the full conjugation of **haber** in all its seven simple tenses is so important for forming compound tenses, it is given here in full. Only the imperfect tense is conjugated regularly, although the imperfect subjunctive is also regular given the unusual form of its base inherited from the 3P–preterit.

**haber,** *has, have, had*

Pres.Part: **habiendo**          Past Part: **habido**

| Pres: | | Pret: | | Fut: | |
|---|---|---|---|---|---|
| he | hemos | hube | hubimos | habré | habrémos |
| has | habéis | hubiste | hubisteis | habrás | habréis |
| ha | han | hubo | hubieron | habrá | habrán |
| **Imp:** | | | | Cond: | |
| **había** | **habíamos** | | | habría | habríamos |
| **habías** | **habíais** | | | habrías | habríais |
| **había** | **habían** | | | habria | habrían |
| Pres.Sub: | | Imp.Sub: | | | |
| haya | hayamos | **hubiera** | **hubiéramos** | | |
| hayas | hayáis | **hubieras** | **hubieráis** | | |
| haya | hayan | **hubiera** | **hubieran** | | |
| | | **or** | | | |
| | | **hubiese** | **hubiésemos** | | |
| | | **hubieses** | **hubieséis** | | |
| | | **hubiese** | **hubiesen** | | |

# The Present Perfect Indicative Tense

Use the appropriate form of **haber** in the *present tense*, followed by the past participle of the desired verb.

In English, this construction is translated with the auxilliary verbs "have" and "has" as in "We have eaten two pancakes, while she has eaten only one."

**haber,** *has, have, had*

| Present Tense | |
|---|---|
| he | hemos |
| has | habéis |
| ha | han |

**+**  **past participle
of desired verb**
(–**ado**/–**ido** ending)

**Examples**

He hablado  con su padre.
> *I have spoken to your father.*

Ella ha comido la manzana.
> *She has eaten the apple.*

Nosotros hemos azido la bandera.
> *We have raised the flag.*

# The Past Perfect Indicative Tense

Use the appropriate form of **haber** in the *imperfect tense*, followed by the past participle of the desired verb.

In English, this construction is translated with the auxilliary verb "had" as in "We had arrived yesterday."

**haber,** *has, have, had*

| Imperfect Tense | |
|---|---|
| había | habíamos |
| habías | habíais |
| había | habían |

**+** past participle
of desired verb
(–ado/–ido ending)

**Examples**

**Había hablado con su padre.**
*I had spoken to your father.*

**Ella había comido la manzana.**
*She had eaten the apple.*

**Nosotros habíamos azido la bandera.**
*We had raised the flag.*

# The Preterit Perfect Indicative Tense

Use the appropriate form of **haber** in the *preterit tense*, followed by the past participle of the desired verb.

The English translations for the past perfect indicative and preterit perfect indicative are the same. The preterit perfect indicative is not as commonly used in conversation as the past perfect indicative.

**haber,** *has, have, had*

| Preterit Tense | |
|---|---|
| hube | hubimos |
| hubiste | hubisteis |
| hubo | hubieron |

**+** **past participle of desired verb** (–**ado**/–**ido** ending)

**Examples**

> **Hube hablado con su padre.**
> *I had spoken to your father.*

> **Ella hubo comido la manzana.**
> *She had eaten the apple.*

> **Nosotros hubimos azido la bandera.**
> *We had raised the flag.*

## The Future Perfect Indicative Tense

Use the appropriate form of **haber** in the *future tense*, followed by the past participle of the desired verb.

    In English, this construction is translated with the auxilliary verbs "will have" as in "We will have read the book by then."

**haber,** *has, have, had*

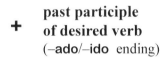

| Future Tense | |
| --- | --- |
| habré | habremos |
| habrás | habréis |
| habrá | habrán |

**+** past participle
of desired verb
(–ado/–ido ending)

**Examples**

    **Yo habré terminado el libro.**
      *I shall have finished the book.*

    **Habré  hablado con su padre antes de la cena.**
      *I will have spoken with your father before dinner.*

    **Cuando usted telefonea, ella habrá  comido la manzana.**
      *When you call, she will have eaten the apple.*

    **Antes del desayuno, nosotros habremos azido la bandera,**
      *We will have raised the flag by breakfast.*

# The Conditional Perfect Indicative Tense

Use the appropriate form of **haber** in the *conditional tense*, followed by the past participle of the desired verb.

In English, this construction is translated with the auxilliary verbs "would have" as in "We would have voted for her."

**haber,** *has, have, had*

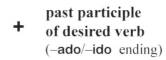

| Conditional Tense | |
|---|---|
| habría | habríamos |
| habrías | habríais |
| habría | habrían |

**+**

**past participle
of desired verb**
(–**ado**/–**ido** ending)

**Examples**

Habría hablado con su padre.
> *I would have spoken to your father.*

Ella habría comido la manzana.
> *She would have eaten the apple.*

Nosotros habríamos azido la bandera.
> *We would have raised the flag.*

# The Present Perfect Subjunctive Tense

Use the appropriate form of **haber** in the *present subjunctive tense,* followed by the past participle of the desired verb.

The use of the subjunctive tense is primarily based upon doubt, denial, wishing or hoping, an emotional response subject to opposing points of view or reactions, future events that may or may not occur, or recommendations.

These basic elements are often intertwined. For example, in many instances an emotional response or speculation is tied with anticipation *and* with events yet to occur. The appearance of the present perfect and pluperfect subjunctive is an extension of the indicative perfect conjugations.

**haber,** *has, have, had*

| Present Subjunctive | |
|---|---|
| haya | hayamos |
| hayas | hayáis |
| haya | hayan |

**+** **past participle of desired verb** (–**ado**/–**ido** ending)

**Examples**

**Dudo que él haya salido.** *I doubt he has left.*

**Es triste que él haya salido.** or
**Es triste que él haya tenido que salir.**
It is sad that he had to leave.

**Niego que él haya salido.**
*I deny that he has left.*

# The Past Perfect Subjunctive Tense

Use the appropriate form of **haber** in the *imperfect subjunctive tense*, followed by the past participle of the desired verb.

**haber,** *has, have, had*

| Imperfect Subjunctive | |
|---|---|
| hubiera | hubiéramos |
| hubieras | hubierais |
| hubiera | hubieran |

**+**

**past participle of desired verb**
(–**ado**/–**ido** ending)

Or the alternative,

**haber,** *has, have, had*

| Imperfect Subjunctive | |
|---|---|
| hubiese | hubiésemos |
| hubieses | hubieseís |
| hubiese | hubiesen |

**+**

**past participle of desired verb**
(–**ado**/–**ido** ending)

**Examples**

The past perfect subjunctive takes the same concepts of the present perfect subjunctive construction and places them in a past context. In the first example below, the speaker is not sure whether the individual had left and, even up to the present moment when the declarations were made, is not sure what happened.

**Dudaba que él hubiera salido.**
*I doubted that he might have left.*

**Negaba que él hubiera salido.**
*I denied that he might have left.*

**Era triste que él hubiera salido.**
*It was sad that he might have left.*

However, if the speaker wishes to affirm that the case is closed, leaving no doubt regarding the outcome, one of the indicative tenses would be used when referring to the past event. For example:

**Dudaba que él había salido.** *I doubted that he had left.*

**Negaba que él había salido.** *I denied he had left.*

**Era triste que él había salido.** *It was sad that he had left .*

The "if clause" shown below is another instance in which the pluperfect subjunctive appears and corroborates the contrary to fact or *future events which may or may not oc*cur nuance of the subjunctive.

**Si él hubiera salido, habríamos estado muy felices.**
*If he would have left, we would have been very happy.*

# Summary of the Seven Compound Tenses

## With cantar (Past Participle: cantado)

| Present Perfect Indicative Tense: | | |
|---|---|---|
| Sing: | he cantado | has cantado | ha cantado |
| Plural: | hemos cantado | habéis cantado | han cantado |
| **Past Perfect Indicative Tense** | | |
| Sing: | había cantado | habías cantado | había cantado |
| Plural: | habíamos cantado | habíais cantado | habían cantado |
| **Preterit Perfect Indicative Tense** | | |
| Sing: | hube cantado | hubiste cantado | hubo cantado |
| Plural: | hubimos cantado | hubisteis cantado | hubieron cantado |
| **Future Perfect Indicative Tense** | | |
| Sing: | habré cantado | habrás cantado | habrá cantado |
| Plural: | habremos cantado | habréis cantado | habrán cantado |
| **Conditional Perfect Indicative Tense** | | |
| Sing: | habría cantado | habrías cantado | habría cantado |
| Plural: | habríamos cantado | habríais cantado | habrían cantado |
| **Present Perfect Subjunctive Tense** | | |
| Sing: | haya cantado | hayas cantado | haya cantado |
| Plural: | hayamos cantado | hayáis cantado | hayan cantado |
| **Past Perfect Subjunctive Tense** | | |
| Sing: | hubiera cantado | hubieras cantado | hubiera cantado |
| Plural: | hubiéramos cantado | hubierais cantado | hubieran cantado |
| **OR** | | |
| Sing: | hubiese cantado | hubieses cantado | hubiese cantado |
| Plural: | hubiésemos cantado | hubieseis cantado | hubiesen cantado |

# Chapter 7

## Other Compound Verb Forms

There are many other compound verb forms that are commonly used in Spanish. For example, a progressive form emphasizes continuing action in progress. The following examples in English illustrate the use of progressive forms.

Examples of progressive forms:

| Present: | I speak |
| Present progressive: | I am speaking. |

| Past: | I spoke. |
| Past progressive: | I was speaking. |

| Future: | I shall speak. |
| Future progressive: | I am going to speak. |

In all three cases, the simple present, past or future in Spanish can be translated into English with either the simple or the progressive forms. Thus:

Simple present:
**Yo hablo.** *I speak,* or *I am speaking.*

Present Progressive:
**Yo estoy hablando.** *I am speaking.*

The progressive is used in Spanish to put emphasis on the action being taken or on the aspect of continuation of the action, and, as in English, it is a compound form requiring two verbs used together.

The present and past progressive moods (not tenses) are formed in Spanish by using the verb **estar** in the present or imperfect tense along with the *present participle* of the action verb. Note that **estar**, like **haber**, is one of the Truly Irregular Verbs, but the only irregularity you will find in these two tenses is the 1S–present ending, **–oy** and the V9 accents in the present tense. The imperfect tense of **estar** is perfectly regular.

## The Present Progressive

For this compound verb form, use the appropriate form of **estar** in the *present tense*, followed by the present participle of the desired verb.

**estar,** *to be*

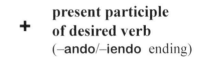

| Present | |
|---------|---------|
| estoy | estamos |
| estás | estáis |
| está | están |

**+** **present participle of desired verb**
(–**ando**/–**iendo** ending)

**Examples**

| | |
|---|---|
| **Estamos comiendo.** | *We are eating.* |
| **¡Estoy hablando!** | *I am speaking!* |

# The Past Progressive

Use the appropriate form of **estar** in the *imperfect tense*, followed by the present participle of the desired verb.

**estar,** *to be*

| Imperfect | |
|---|---|
| estaba | estábamos |
| estabas | estabais |
| estaba | estaban |

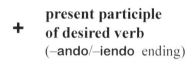

**+**  **present participle of desired verb** (–**ando**/–**iendo** ending)

**Examples**

| | |
|---|---|
| **Estábamos comiendo.** | We were eating. |
| **¡Estaba hablando!** | I was speaking! |

# The Future Progressive

To construct the future progressive, use the appropriate form of **ir** in the *present tense*, followed by the preposition **a** and the infinitive of the desired verb.

The English translation for the future progressive uses the phrase "going to." This gives the action a future aspect as an action that has not yet begun. Of course, **ir** is also one of the Truly Irregular Verbs. Its conjugation in the present tense is given below.

**ir,** *to go*

| present ||
|---------|---------|
| **voy** | **vamos** |
| **vas** | **vais** |
| **va**  | **van**  |

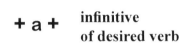

**Examples**

**Vamos a comer.**   *We are going to eat.*
                    or *"Let's eat."*

**¡Voy a hablar!**   *I am going to speak!*

**Va a escribir el cuento.**
          *She is going to write the story.*

**¿Van ustedes a ir al centro?**
          *Are you-all going to go downtown?*

# Continuous Unending Action

There is also a compound form that uses either the present or imperfect tense of the verb **ir** without the preposition **a**. The distinction here is of an action that seems to go on without end, and its use is not particularly complimentary. The action might be translated with the phrase "kept right on...."

To create this mood, use the appropriate form of **ir** in either the *present tense or the imperfect tense,* and the present participle of the desired verb.

**ir,** *to go*

| Present | |
|---------|---------|
| **voy** | **vamos** |
| **vas** | **vais** |
| **va** | **van** |

**+** **present participle of desired verb** (–**ando**/–**iendo** ending)

**ir,** *to go*

| Imperfect | |
|-----------|---------|
| **iba** | **íbamos** |
| **ibas** | **ibais** |
| **iba** | **iban** |

**+** **present participle of desired verb** (–**ando**/–**iendo** ending)

**Examples**

| | |
|---|---|
| **Va hablando.** | *She keeps right on talking.* (present tense) |
| **Él iba hablando.** | *He kept right on talking.* (past tense) |

# Recently Completed Action

Actions that have recently been completed are often recognized in English with the word "just," as in "I have just eaten." or "I have just finished eating." This form implies a completed action. A common Spanish construction is to use the present tense of **acabar** *to finish, to complete* and the preposition **de** with the infinitive of the action verb. Thus "I have just eaten." becomes **Acabo de comer**.

To describe recently completed action, use the appropriate form of **acabar** in the *present tense*, followed by the preposition **de** and the infinitive of the desired verb.

**acabar,** *to complete*

| present | |
|---------|---------|
| acabo | acábamos |
| acabas | acabáis |
| acaba | acaban |

**+ de +**   **infinitive of desired verb**

**Examples**

> **Acabo de leer ese libro.**
> *I have just finished reading that book.*

> **¡Acaban de llegar!**   *They have just arrived!*

# Conclusion

For the non-native speaker, learning to use Spanish verbs correctly in all their many tenses and forms is not an easy task. Dealing with the hundreds of irregular verbs without some clearly defined framework within which to classify them makes that task even more difficult.

By committing the ten spelling rules and ten vowel variations presented in this book to memory and understanding how they work, you will have gone a long way toward achieving a higher degree of fluency in Spanish than you might have thought possible. Instead of memorizing hundreds of seemingly unrelated verb irregularities, you will have reduced the task to a mere nineteen Truly Irregular Verbs with which to contend.

Much practice and frequent review of the verb lists in this book will be necessary before you can feel fully at ease using Spanish verbs. But the end result is surely worth the effort.

.